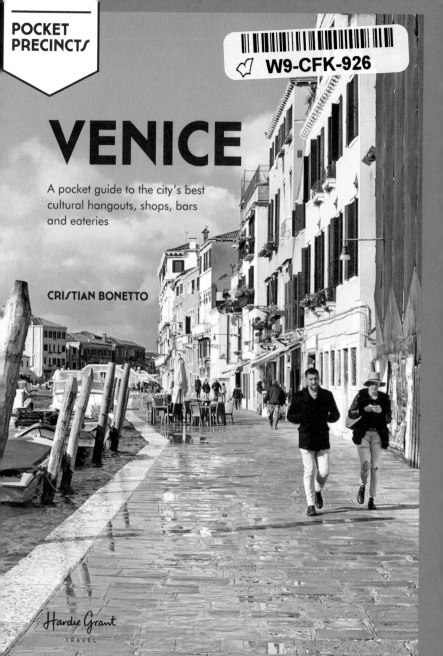

POCKET
PRECINCTS

W9-CFK-926

VENICE

A pocket guide to the city's best
cultural hangouts, shops, bars
and eateries

CRISTIAN BONETTO

Hardie Grant
TRAVEL

CONTENTS

LV63232

INTRODUCTION

The world is flooded with drop-dead gorgeous cities. Yet none trump Venice. For centuries, the famous and infamous have swiped right on La Serenissima (The Most Serene Republic). Henry III declared that if he were not King of France, he would choose to be a citizen of Venice. Truman Capote likened it to eating an entire box of chocolate liqueurs in one go, while Marcel Proust compared the city to a dream. The appeal is instant and hypnotic: an improbable, real-life fairytale of lacework palazzi (palaces), glittering basilicas and moody, hushed canals moored with peeling boats and gondolas. Labyrinthine, Escher-minded calli (streets) disorientate and surprise, leading to an embarrassment of riches, from whole suites of Tintoretto paintings to medieval mosaics made of gold. Here, Byzantine domes, Moorish windows and spice-laced local dishes speak of a city at the crossroads of East and West; the cosmopolitan capital of a once mighty maritime republic that gave the world Marco Polo, Vivaldi and playboy Casanova.

Yet, just like the sea on which it floats, Venice is a creature both familiar and mysterious. There is the Venice of world-famous landmarks, queuing visitors and Made-in-China souvenirs, and then there is the Venice of the venexiani (Venetians). Both cities intersect, yet they remain separate entities. While the former can feel like an Old-World Disneyland, the latter is living, dynamic and nuanced. *Venice Pocket Precincts* is a portal into the Venezia lived by the locals, a complex town both fiercely traditional and boldly creative. This guide carves Venice into nine navigable precincts, each featuring a selection of outstanding sights, eateries, bars, shops and more. The cut is decisively selective; handpicked highlights that both I and my Venetian friends prize. Some are famous, many are not. Together, they reveal a world of soul-stirring brushstrokes and secret artisan studios, of sustainable restaurants and locavore wine bars, of street art, vineyards, and sleepy bucolic landscapes. Recently battered by unsustainable tourism, record floods and a pandemic, Venice, more than ever, deserves respect and reverence. Tread lightly, support local and watch La Serenissima let down her guard and reveal her true self to you.

Cristian Bonetto

A PERFECT VENICE DAY

My perfect day in Venice begins with morning strudel, caffè (coffee) and banter at veteran **Pasticceria Rizzardini**. From here, I happily dive into the colours and aromas of the nearby **Mercato di Rialto**. If I'm feeling cheeky, I might pop into **All'Arco** for a morning prosecco (completely normal in this town) before taking in the view from the **Ponte di Rialto** (Rialto Bridge) – a scene that never gets old. Bridge crossed, I hop onto a San Marco–bound number 1 vaporetto (ferry), picking out my favourite palazzi (palaces) as we sail down the Grand Canal. The view of the **Basilica di Santa Maria della Salute** is a fool-proof pick-me-up, and my cue to get ready to disembark. Alighting at San Marco (Giardinetti), I make a quick pit-stop at the **Giardini Reali** for a splash of green before continuing to the **Palazzo Ducale**, ticket pre-booked online to avoid the longest queues. I spend the rest of the morning roaming the palace, lost in epic artworks and tales of political intrigue. Of course, it wouldn't be a perfect day without stepping into adjoining **Piazza San Marco** to swoon over the city's most celebrated building, the **Basilica di San Marco**. If I need another caffeine hit, I'll join locals in the back bar at time-warped **Caffè Florian**. Next, I head east along waterfront Riva degli Schiavonì, nodding to Palladio's **Chiesa di San Giorgio Maggiore** across the water. I'll have already reserved a table at campo-side **Al Covo**, where a long, lazy lunch of local seafood feels well earned. Whiskers licked, I spend the rest of the afternoon lazily ambling the low-key streets of Castello. This usually involves admiring the Arsenale's Renaissance **Porta Magna** and perusing the neighbourhood's independent shops and artisan studios. Personal favourites include **Atelier Alessandro Merlin** and **Ceramiche Chimera** for unique contemporary ceramics. Once evening descends, I head across to Cannaregio for canal-side aperitivo and people watching at **Al Timon** or **Vino Vero**, usually devouring enough cicheti (Venetian tapas) to call it dinner. If the night is still young, a nightcap calls at the always fun **Osteria da Filo.**

Isola Carbonera

Laguna   Veneta

Isola di Tessera

VENICE

Isola Campalto

MURANO

Isola di
San Secondo

8

CANNAREGIO

ISOLA DI
SAN MICHELE

2

4   **3**

Isola
delle
Tresse

SANTA CROCE   SAN
POLO

6

DORSODURO   SAN
MARCO   **1**

CASTELLO

5

Sant'Elena

GIUDECCA   **7**

ISOLA DI
SAN GIORGIO
MAGGIORE

Isola di
San Sèrvolo

La Grazia

Isola Buel del Lovo

TORCELLO

Isola di Mazzorbetto

(9)

MAZZORBO **BURANO**

Isola della Madonna del Monte

Isola ex Ridotto di Crevan

Isola di San Francesco del Deserto

Isola di San Giacomo in Paludo

Lazzaretto Nuovo

Isola di Sant'Erasmo

gnole

Lido di Venezia

PRECINCT/

FIELD TRIP/

ƆAN MARCO

Home to Venice's most famous basilica, palace and square, San Marco is big on star power. Lively, narrow, oft-disorientating calli (streets) lead to a string of superlatives, from Venice's finest Byzantine mosaics to its largest painting, grandest theatre, oldest cafe and most legendary bars. The sestiere (district) spans the tangle of streets between Venice's two most famous landmarks: the Ponte di Rialto (Rialto Bridge) and Piazza San Marco. The latter is the city's alfresco salotto (living room), lorded over by the fusion curves of the Basilica di San Marco (*see* p. 2) and arched façades of the Procuratie (Procuracies, *see* p. 6). Sidled up against the basilica is Palazzo Ducale (*see* p. 4), from where doges once ruled a republic that reached Cyprus. This is a neighbourhood long accustomed to power, wealth and fame, its palace halls, coffee houses and Grand-Canal bars entertaining everyone from French emperors to Hollywood deities.

Shops, bacari (wine bars) and restaurants fill the streets north and west of Piazza San Marco, with high-end galleries, boutiques, hotels and world-famous cocktail dens – among them Harry's Bar and Bar Longhi (*see* p. 17) – cranking up the glam between Piazza San Marco and sun-drenched Campo San Stefano to the west. And while such fame does come at a cost – high prices, long queues, torrents of tourists – forward planning and a discerning hit list might just leave you smitten too.

→ *View of Isola di San Giorgio Maggiore from outside Palazzo Ducale*

1 BA*I*LICA DI *I*AN MARCO

Piazza San Marco
041 270 8311
[MAP p. 163 D2]

Modelled on Constantinople's Church of the Holy Apostles, crowned by Arabesque domes, and lavished with around 8,000 square metres (86,000 square feet) of Byzantine mosaics, no building captures Venice's cosmopolitan pedigree like St Mark's Basilica. It was founded in the 9th century as the final resting place for St Mark the Evangelist, his corpse smuggled out of Egypt in a barrel of pork fat. The tale is recounted in four of the lunette mosaics above the portals, the oldest, from 1270, on the far left. The four horses (Quadriga) above the entrance are copies of the Graeco–Roman originals displayed in the basilica's **museum**, trophies from the Sack of Constantinople in 1204. Inside, three tesserae-encrusted domes depict the Pentecost, Ascension and Prophets. The basilica is free, but it's worth paying to view the jewel-studded Pala d'Oro altarpiece, **treasury** and museum, home to manuscripts, tapestries and Crusades-era spoils. In summer, secure 'Skip the Line' basilica tickets (basilicasanmarco.it).

POCKET TIP

Opening hours are notoriously changeable in Italy so always check ahead. Some churches close for lunch while many attractions and shops keep longer opening hours in the summer months or from April to October.

POCKET TIP

While the views from the basilica's campanile (bell tower) are spectacular, skip it for the even better views and thinner crowds at San Giorgio Maggiore (see p. 102), if the queues are long.

2 PALAZZO DUCALE

Piazzetta San Marco 1
041 271 5911
[MAP p. 163 E3]

For centuries, candy-coloured Palazzo Ducale was the epicentre of Venetian power, home to the city's rulers, government, courts and prison. Although the doge's official residence since around the 10th century, the current Gothic–Renaissance confection dates from the 14th century. The palace remains a sucker punch of Venetian vanity and flair, with a feast of frescoes, canvases and carvings. In the magnificent Renaissance courtyard, Jacopo Sansovino's statues of Mars and Neptune – guarding the monumental Staircase of the Giants – symbolise the Republic's domination of land and sea. Upstairs, gilded chambers drip with depictions of Venetian prowess, like Vittore Carpaccio's *The Lion of St Mark* and Paolo Veronese's *Juno Bestowing Her Gifts on Venice*. Veronese depicts the city crowned by Victory in the gargantuan Great Council Chamber, also home to one of the world's largest oil paintings, *Il Paradiso*, by Tintoretto and son Domenico Robusti. It's all in stark contrast to the prison cells downstairs, accessed via the infamous **Bridge of Sighs**.

POCKET TIP

Buy your Palazzo Ducale ticket online (palazzoducale.visitmuve.it) to avoid long queues and join a Secret Itineraries tour to view secret passageways and the prison cell from which Casanova escaped with help from a monk.

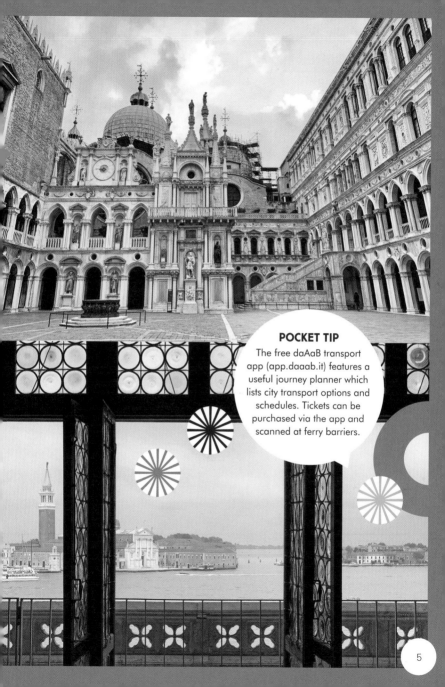

POCKET TIP

The free daAaB transport app (app.daaab.it) features a useful journey planner which lists city transport options and schedules. Tickets can be purchased via the app and scanned at ferry barriers.

5

3 MU⌠EO CORRER

Piazza San Marco 52
041 240 5211
[MAP p.162 B3]

When control of Venice switched from Austrian to French hands in 1806, Emperor Napoleon decided on Piazza San Marco to build his new Venetian maison (house). Numerous buildings, including the 16th-century Chiesa di San Geminiano, were torn down in the process, closing off the piazza and connecting the 16th-century Procuratie Vecchie (Old Procuracies) on the northern side of the square to the Procuratie Nuove (New Procuracies) on the south. Today, Napoleon's wing and the Procuratie Nuove form the Museo Correr, a treasure trove of artefacts showcasing Venetian power and culture. The historic maps and atlases are especially fascinating and I always manage to find new details in Jacopo de' Barbari's woodblock perspective of late-15-century Venice. Then there's the **Biblioteca Nazionale Marciana**'s reading room, a breathtaking hall decorated with frescoes by Veronese, Titian and Tintoretto. The museum gift shop, reached via the monumental staircase leading up to the museum and accessible without a museum ticket, is one of the city's best.

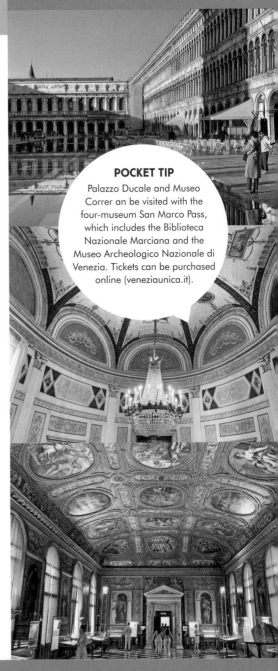

POCKET TIP
Palazzo Ducale and Museo Correr an be visited with the four-museum San Marco Pass, which includes the Biblioteca Nazionale Marciana and the Museo Archeologico Nazionale di Venezia. Tickets can be purchased online (veneziaunica.it).

POCKET TIP

Lovers of fashion and textiles can fawn over stunning frocks, fabrics and tapestries at moody Palazzo Fortuny (Campo San Beneto 3958), former home and studio of Art-Nouveau designer Mariano Fortuny y Madrazo.

4 TEATRO LA FENICE

Campo San Fantin 1977
041 78 66 75
[MAP p. 173 C2]

Nobody takes its name as seriously as Venice's magnificent opera house. Named La Fenice (The Phoenix) after replacing fire-ravaged Teatro San Benedetto in 1792, La Fenice itself went up in flames twice; in 1836 and 1996. Milanese architect Aldo Rossi oversaw the theatre's last reconstruction, even using stills from Luchino Visconti's film *Senso* to study its interior. Re-opened in late 2003, his €90-million replica could fool most, its Rococo-inspired sweep of boxes, sconces and paintings capturing the pomp and glamour of opera's gilded age. Opera season usually runs from November to July and from September to October, and catching a performance here is unforgettable, as much for the atmosphere as for any aria. Alternatively, simply drop in for a self-guided tour of the remarkable space, especially ideal on a rainy day. Access the audio tour via the free La Fenice app or grab an audio guide at the theatre (bring photo ID).

5 POLI DISTILLERIE

Campiello Feltrina 2511b
041 866 0104
[MAP p. 173 B3]

Grappa is as quintessentially settentrionale (northern Italian) as polenta, speck and fog. And proper grappa tastes nothing like the backyard rocket fuel you may have swilled back home. The Poli family have been distilling the good stuff since 1898, and their store in Venice is a showcase for all that is smooth and aromatic about pomace brandy. You'll find everything from spritely new grappe to sultry, honey-like barrique options aged in French oak. If grappa isn't your thing, check out Poli's artisanal vermouth, liqueurs and amaro, the latter infused with over 30 varieties of herbs. I rarely leave town without a bottle of their Marconi 46 gin. Made with herbs from Asiago plateau north-west of Venice, it's intense, botanical and fabulous spiked with a sprig of rosemary. For €3 (€5 with a traditional snack) you can sample three products of your choice, reimbursed if you make a purchase.

6 MATERIALMENTE

Mercerie San Salvador 4850
041 528 6881
[MAP p. 166 A4]

It was a search for studio space that reunited old school friends Maddalena Venier and Alessandro Salvadori. These days, not only do they share a work space in Giudecca, they also share this tiny store, filled with their handmade sculptures, lamps and jewellery. Theirs is a fantastical world, where ladder-shaped plants sprout out of houses and where pirate ships sail between crescent moons and coupled whales. Add silhouetted Gothic palaces, cute rocking birds and giant hanging fish and it's easy to feel that you're tripping like a magic realist. Playfully patterned pendant lights add colour, while the contemporary jewellery is unapologetically individualistic. Prices are fair for the work involved: €50 to €150 for rings, around €100 for earrings and €140 for a pendant lamp. Metalwork sculptures vary in price, ranging from around €130 for a smaller piece to a few hundred euro for larger, more elaborate creations.

7 THE MERCHANT OF VENICE

Campo San Fantin
041 296 0559
[MAP p. 173 C2]

Legend has it that Byzantine princess Theodora Anna Doukaina – wife of Doge Domenico Selvo – first introduced Venice to perfumery in the 11th century. Her toiletry habits soon became a hit with Venetian noblewomen and by the 16th century, the city had established itself as a perfume-making hub. The tradition lives on at this luxe Venetian perfumery, its flagship store occupying a neo-Gothic pharmacy by architect Giambattista Meduna (designer of the second La Fenice theatre). It's a time-warped affair, with beautiful detailing that includes walnut panelling, allegorical terracotta statues of botany, medicine, surgery and physics, and a central counter bas-relief depicting a distillation laboratory. The locally made perfumes, toiletries and home fragrances find their muse in Venetian landmarks, history and culture. These include eau de parfums inspired by La Fenice and a series of fragrances bottled in Murano glass. Those wanting to stay south of €30 can opt for heady shower gels, shampoos, conditioners and lotions.

POCKET TIP

If you're in Cannaregio, peer into The Merchant of Venice's other branch at Strada Nova 2233a, housed in an 18th-century apothecary.

11

8 RO/A /ALVA

Calle Fiubera 951
041 521 0544
[MAP p. 162 C1]

Despite its proximity to Piazza San Marco, stalwart pasticceria Rosa Salva is no tourist trap. Locals are as common as out-of-towners, downing well-brewed espresso, grabbing a quick bite, or taking home a vassoio di dolci (tray of sweets). Mornings are always brighter with one of their buttery brioche alla mela (baked apple pastry) in hand, my morning staple here. That said, it's difficult to go wrong. The counter is a Technicolor triumph, neatly lined with just-baked pastries, luscious bignè (profiteroles), zuppa inglese (liqueur-dipped ladyfingers) and creamy cups of tiramisu. Come lunchtime, opt for their standout tramezzini, mini sandwiches filled with anything from egg and asparagus, to grilled pork and eggplant, wafer-thin prosciutto and shrimps. While tables are available, most locals refuel al banco (standing at the bar), where prices are cheaper. Before leaving, check out the range of take-home goods, which include gorgeous house-made jams and Venetian biscotti.

POCKET TIP

Avoid fines by not feeding pigeons, picnicking on streets, squares and bridges, carrying/riding bikes through the city centre, lying down on public benches or purchasing from roaming street vendors.

9 GELATOTECA SUSO

Calle della Bissa 5453
348 564 6545
[MAP p. 166 B3]

Suso's side-street location is no ruse for the hordes queuing to lick the city's best gelato. Mercifully, the line moves fast and before you know it, you're at the counter. This, at least for me, is the hard part: what to choose from a sweep of luscious, seasonal gusti (flavours)? While their iterations of classics like hazelnut, stracciatella and lemon are gorgeous, it's the more experimental house specialties that draw me here. Drool over glossy tarta de queso (cheesecake gelato layered with butter biscuit and smothered in a wild-strawberry coulis), bagigi peanut (peanut-butter cream pimped with salted peanuts, caramel and sweet salt from Cervia) or the Manet, a posh combo of salted pistachio and gianduja (hazelnut-infused chocolate). If you're done with cups and cones (gluten-free cones are on standby), order a panino di Suso, gelato served in a panettone sandwich. Better than sex.

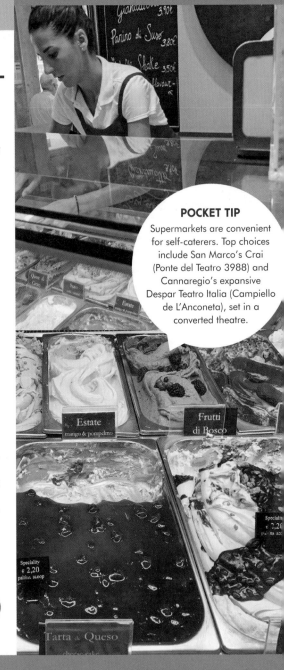

POCKET TIP

Supermarkets are convenient for self-caterers. Top choices include San Marco's Crai (Ponte del Teatro 3988) and Cannaregio's expansive Despar Teatro Italia (Campiello de L'Anconeta), set in a converted theatre.

10 BACARANDO IN CORTE DELL'ORSO

Corte Dell'Orso 5495
041 523 8280
[MAP p. 166 B3]

Despite its furtive location – down an inconspicuous alley off the northern end of Campo San Bortolomeo – Bacarando is rarely short of a crowd. Peeps scurry here for the fancy cicheti (Venetian tapas), lined up like Insta-worthy artworks behind the counter. You'll find meat, fish and vegetable-based options, from grilled polenta topped with calamari and sugo (tomato sauce) to guiltily good mozzarella in carrozza (crumbed, deep-fried mozzarella). The spiedini (skewers) – snack-format versions of classic dishes like insalata caprese (mozzarella, tomato and basil salad) – are handy bar bites, though I rarely miss their tortini, potato-and-cream-based 'little cakes' topped with marinated vegetables, hard-boiled eggs and more. There's a solid selection of wines by the glass, plus more space than your regular bacaro (wine bar). Check Bacarando's Facebook page for upcoming music gigs, usually rolled out Wednesday and Sunday evenings.

POCKET TIP

Department store Fondaco dei Tedeschi (Calle del Fontego dei Tedeschi) offers spectacular views of Venice and – on clear days – the Alps from its free rooftop terrace. Reserve online (dfs.com/en/venice/t-fondaco-rooftop-terrace).

POCKET TIP

Slightly cheaper than its more glamorous rival Bar Longhi, Hotel Monaco & Grand Canal (Calle Vallaresso) also offers a waterfront terrace with stunning Grand Canal views.

11 BAR LONGHI

Gritti Palace Hotel
Campo Santa Maria del Giglio
2467
041 79 46 11
[MAP p. 173 C3]

Whenever I'm in a recklessly decadent mood, I make an impromptu appearance at Bar Longhi. Granted, well-mixed cocktails here hover in the €20s, but the pay-off is sheer escapism. The bar sits inside the 15th-century Palazzo Pisani Gritti, former pad of doge Andrea Gritti and current home of Venice's grandest hotel, the Gritti Palace. Ernest Hemingway finished his novel *Across the River and into the Trees* while slumbering here. He also spent many an hour working up hangovers at its ground-floor bar, home to three original paintings by its namesake, 18th-century artist Pietro Longhi. And while British wordsmith W. Somerset Maugham rightfully praised the bar's waterfront terrace and basilica views, I prefer hunkering down inside, where cushy emerald-hued sofas, Murano-glass sconces and etched antique mirrors set a snug scene for quiet afternoons reading or eavesdropping on the lives and petit dramas of the one per cent.

17

12 CAFFÈ FLORIAN

Piazza San Marco 57
041 520 5641
[MAP p. 162 C3]

Some of history's most famous (and infamous) have sipped at the Florian: scandal-mongers Casanova and Oscar Wilde, screen queens Grace Kelly and Katherine Hepburn, fashion deity Coco Chanel, even pop maverick Andy Warhol. Not so much a cafe as a Venetian institution, it's the oldest continuously operating cafe in the world, trading on Piazza San Marco since December 1720. The current fit-out dates from the mid-19th century, its elegant rooms awash with frescoes, stuccos, velvet and mirrors fit for a royal boudoir. Old-school glamour extends to the service: suited waiters, silver serving trays and an afternoon orchestra to boot (leave your flip-flops, hot pants and tank tops at your hotel). Of course, such trimmings come with a hefty price tag; piazza seating during concerts is an extra €6 per adult. If you're not too fussed about piazza-side posing, sip on your feet in the cheaper back bar, where your drink of choice should be Florian's rightly famous hot chocolate.

POCKET TIP

Commissioned by Napoleon and wedged between Piazza San Marco and the waterfront, the restored Giardini Reali (Royal Gardens; Fondamenta dei Giardini) provide a handy green escape close to major sights.

CANNAREGIO

Synagogues, off-the-beaten-track Renaissance masterpieces and canal-side aperitivi lure the cognoscenti to Venice's northernmost sestiere (district). While most tourists stick to souvenir-riddled Strada Nova – part of the pedestrian freeway linking the train station to the Ponte di Rialto (Rialto Bridge) – those in the know slip into the quieter calli (streets) shooting north of it. It's these streets that lead to the superlative waterfront bacari (wine bars) of Fondamenta dei Ormesini, packed nightly with beer and vino-swilling creatives, students, families and clued-in out-of-towners. Further north, across another two of Cannaregio's rectilinear canals, lies the Gothic Chiesa della Madonna dell'Orto (*see* p. 22), final resting place of Tintoretto and home to two of his most monumental works. At the eastern end of the sestiere lies another Renaissance treasure, the polychromatic Chiesa di Santa Maria dei Miracoli (*see* p. 23).

Kippers and kosher cappuccini await on and around Campo de Gheto Novo, heart of the Jewish Ghetto. Decreed in the early 16th century, this is Europe's oldest Ghetto, its high-rise tenements indicative of a (once) walled-off community forced to build up instead of out. South of Strada Nova are Cannaregio's Grand Canal palazzi (palaces). Among them is Ca' d'Oro (*see* p. 24), home to masterpieces that include Titian's revered depiction of *Venus with a Mirror*. Adding to the neighbourhood's artistic appeal is a sprinkling of small galleries and artisan studios on the side streets and 'outer canal banks', among them the world-famous, tech-resistant printer, Gianni Basso (*see* p. 26).

→ *Contemporary installation at Galleria Giorgio Franchetti alla Ca' d'Oro*

1 CHIESA DELLA MADONNA DELL'ORTO

Campo de la Madonna
dell'Orto 3520
041 71 99 33
[MAP p. 177 E2]

This red-brick beauty is one of Venice's standout Gothic buildings. Founded in the mid-14th-century and originally dedicated to St Christopher (that's him above the entrance with the Virgin and the Archangel Gabriel), the church was renamed Madonna dell'Orto (Madonna of the Vegetable Garden) in honour of a miraculous statue of the Virgin, found in a neighbouring patch of produce. The church was Tintoretto's local parish and art lovers stop here to view two of his finest works (without the crowds): *Presentation of the Virgin in the Temple* and *Last Judgment*. It's an especially apt location for the Renaissance masterpieces given the church is also Tintoretto's final resting place; you'll find his tomb to the right of the altar.

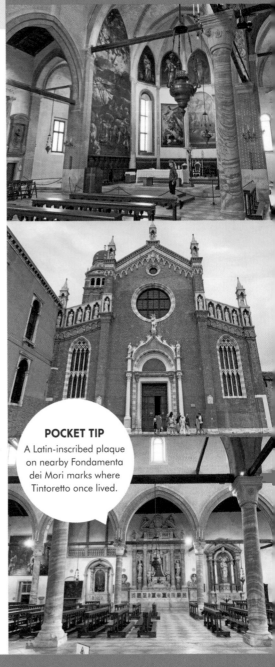

POCKET TIP

A Latin-inscribed plaque on nearby Fondamenta dei Mori marks where Tintoretto once lived.

2 CHIESA DI SANTA MARIA DEI MIRACOLI

Campo dei Miracoli 6074
041 523 5293
[MAP p. 166 C2]

Pietro Lombardo knew how to mix and match, creating this polychromatic centrepiece using marble from the slag heaps of the Basilica di San Marco. The architect's late-15th-century Church of St Mary of the Miracles was built to house a miraculously weeping icon of the Virgin and Child, painted by Zanino di Pietro. The dry-eyed icon still lurks inside, a tender work exemplifying the transition of artistic style from Byzantine to Gothic. Note the sea creatures and angels on the pillars flanking the chancel, chiseled by Lombardo's equally famous sons, Tullio and Antonio Lombardo. Looking down on it all are ceiling portraits of prophets and patriarchs, sporting Venetian garb and commonly attributed to Renaissance painter Pier Maria Pennacchi and his collaborators. Architecturally speaking, the buttress-free barrel-vaulted ceiling is considered a triumph of Renaissance engineering.

3 GALLERIA GIORGIO FRANCHETTI ALLA CA' D'ORO

Calle di Ca' d'Oro 3932
041 520 0345
[MAP p. 169 E1]

The 15th-century 'Golden House' was named for the gold-leaf that once adorned its delicate Gothic façade. The glitter may have faded, but the palace still dazzles with its jewel-box art and loggia (balcony) views of the Grand Canal. Top billing goes to Titian's *Venus with a Mirror* and Andrea Mantegna's *San Sebastiano*, the latter ominously warning that 'Nothing is stable if not divine. The rest is smoke'. Anthony van Dyck's Portrait of Marcello Durazzo is one of the Flemish star's finest works, dashingly depicting a Genoese nobleman. Look out for Gian Lorenzo Bernini's allegorical terracotta models, used when designing his landmark fountain for Rome's Piazza Navona. The gallery itself is named for Baron Giorgio Franchetti, who bequeathed the palace and his art collection to Venice in 1916. His ashes lie beneath a purple porphyry column in the mosaic-floored court downstairs.

4 MUSEO EBRAICO & SYNAGOGUES TOUR

Campo de Gheto Novo 2902
041 71 53 59
[MAP p. 176 B2]

Triumph, tradition and tribulation underscore the Museo Ebraico (Jewish Museum). A porthole into the long, storied history of Venice's Jewish community, it focuses on the different Jewish groups that settled in the Ghetto through to the dark days of World War II. While its inventory is relatively small, the museum contains some beautiful pieces, including Renaissance-era texts, meticulous embroidery and fine Venetian silverware. The true highlight, however, is the 40-minute guided tour of historic Ghetto synagogues, offered in Italian and English and departing hourly on the half hour. The rotating hit list includes the early 16th-century **Scuola Canton**, unique for its eight biblically-themed paintings (a rare feature in synagogues) and the magnificent, Baldassare Longhena-designed **Scuola Spagnola**, the largest of the Ghetto's synagogues. My personal favourite is the jewel-box **Scuola Grande Tedesca**, its elliptical women's gallery lending a theatrical touch.

5 GIANNI BA*SS*O

Calle del Fumo 5306
041 523 4681
[MAP p. 178 C4]

Gianni Basso is the rock star of artisanal printing. Pre-industrial presses, hand-carved wood printing blocks and other rare objects fill his workshop and miniature print museum, among them incised plates from the first printing of *Pinocchio*. With son Stefano, he produces distinctive invitations, bookplates, books, old maps and more. The proud Venetian was one of the last apprentices to be taught by the city's Armenian monks, famed for the beauty and precision of their printing. Their legacy lives on in Gianni's work, which also includes custom business cards favoured by international celebrities, politicians and royalty. Expect to pay around €95 for 100 business cards, and much less for postcards and bookmarks. Custom stationery orders usually take about three days though you'll need to actually visit the workshop to place an order; Gianni is unapologetically old-school, with no website, but international shipping is available.

6 FEELIN' VENICE

Strada Nova 4194
041 887 8639
[MAP p. 169 F1]

Feelin' Venice is a big FU to the glut of tacky souvenir shops marring the city. Instead of 'Venice' baseball caps and 'Mob Boss' tees, you'll find a useful mix of design-literate items, from hardback notebooks and recycled-graphite pencils, to coffee mugs, postcards and posters. All are printed with playful, Venice-themed artwork by young, local graphic artists, among them Feelin' Venice co-founder Filippo Soffrizzi. You'll also find totes, drawstring bags and tees, made with good-quality, organic cotton. Not only is it a great spot to pick up cool, city-themed gifts, it's also a way of showing solidarity with Venetian artists and artisans in their battle against foreign-made, mass-produced junk and crippling rents. Considering the uniqueness of the items, prices are reasonable, with most items below €20.

POCKET TIP

There's another branch of Feelin' Venice at Calle de la Mandola 3720 in San Marco.

7 PLUM PLUM CREATION/

Fondamenta dei Ormesini 2681
041 476 5404
[MAP p. 176 C2]

Plum Plum Creations is the studio-gallery of talented Arianna Sautariello (and her pup Bic). Honing her printmaking skills at the Accademia di Belle Arti di Venezia, the young artist has developed a loyal following for her colourful, upbeat linocuts, etchings and watercolours of Venetian palaces, canals and bridges. There's a storybook quality to the work, which finds its inspiration in both personal photographs and online images. Prices are democratic, ranging from loose-change bookmarks and postcards, to affordable prints and more expensive original works. Arianna also runs printmaking courses in Italian and English. Options include four-hour courses, best booked a few days in advance; check online (plumplumcreations.com) for updated times and prices. Short printmaking demonstrations are also available on request. Best of all, the studio sits on one of Venice's most vibrant aperitivo strips, which means post-shopping brindisi (toasts), bites and people watching are at your feet.

8 SULLALUNA

Fondamenta Misericordia 2535
041 72 29 24
[MAP p. 177 E3]

Cafe, bistro and bookstore in one, 'On the Moon' is the kind of place we all wish we had at the end of our street. I love the freshly picked flowers, the illustrated books for sale and the clipboard menu of light, organic, vegetarian bites. It's a welcome switch from the city's heavier traditional fare, with options like herb focaccia filled with fluffy ricotta and artichoke hearts and made-from-scratch baked goods like spelt, chocolate and pear cake. Small producers are also championed on the wine list, which includes the owners' own organic Prosecco DOCG, Lunatico (meaning 'Moody'), made in the Veneto hamlet of Refrontolo. Alternatively, you can guzzle organic bottled beers and juices, herbal teas and chai latte. On sunny days, you'll find me chilling by the water with a platter of local cheeses, a glass of Malvasia and my latest picture-book purchase. It's the simple things.

29

9 PASTICCERIA DAL MAS

Rio Terà Lista di Spagna
149–150a
041 71 51 01
[MAP p. 170 B1]

There are few worthy pit-stops near the train station, but Pasticceria Dal Mas is one of them. A soothing childhood scene of espresso-brewing matriarchs and mission-brown panelling, the place has been run by the Balestra family since 1965. Counters bait locals and visitors alike with their fragrant, made-from-scratch treats. These include an impressive range of morning brioche, all-day pastine (bite-sized pastries) and crunchy Venetian biscotti. The coffee is equally good (not always the case in Venice), with smooth, velvety espresso and competent cappucini. Closer to lunch, order a spritz and pair with a just-baked quiche, golden salatini (pastry dough stuffed with vegetables, cheese or meat) or moreish pizzetta (mini pizza). If chocolate makes you purr, check out Dal Mas' dedicated chocolate shop next door, which peddles some of the finest cocoa concoctions in town. The Venice-themed chocolate tins are especially handy for those seeking gifts for gluttons back home.

POCKET TIP

Drop by kosher bakery Panificio Giovanni Volpe (Calle del Ghetto Vecchio 1143) for Ghetto specialties like impada, an elongated, sugar-dusted biscuit made with ground almonds.

PASTICCERIA DAL MAS

10 AL TIMON

Fondamenta dei Ormesini 2754
041 524 6066
[MAP p. 176 C2]

Evergreen bacaro (wine bar) Al Timon has the lot: top-notch local vino, quality bites, fun crowds, even a moored barge for patrons in the summer. The dirt-cheap crostini (small open-faced sandwiches) are fresh, creative and seasonal, topped with anything from smoked ricotta with berries and balsamic vinegar to pancetta (salt-cured pork belly) with pumpkin. If you're especially famished, the place is also famous for its bistecca alla fiorentina (Florentine steak) that comes in huge, juicy slabs big enough for two. Served on a wooden tagliere (platter) with fried potatoes and other vegetables, the steaks are served rare. While you can request yours well done, expect push back; a bloodless bistecca alla fiorentina is culinary sacrilege. Tip: whether heading in for cicheti (tapas) or a carnivorous feast at a table, go early to dodge the longest queues and wait times.

11 TORREFAZIONE CANNAREGIO

Fondamenta dei Ormesini 2804
041 71 63 71
[MAP p. 176 B2]

Coffee snobs find their tribe at this canal-side roaster-cafe, whose offerings include that ever-elusive antipodean flat white coffee. Despite being around since 1930, the business has moved with the times. Classic espresso is offered alongside Third-Wave brewing techniques like V60 and Bunn filter, while the rotating selection of beans includes both special blends and single origins. Best of all, the coffee is sourced ethically. Teas and hot chocolate are on standby, while edibles include plump cornetti (Italian croissants) and glossy, sticky tarts I rarely resist. And while there's no shortage of locals dropping in for a quick stand-up swill at the bar, retro sofas, tables and free wi-fi make this a good place to linger. If the sun is out and you're in luck, you might even score one of the waterside tables.

POCKET TIP

If cornetti (Italian croissants) don't cut it for breakfast, tuck into granola, energy bowls, bagels, avocado toast and smoothies at globally minded cafe-bar Combo (Campo dei Gesuiti 4878).

12 VINO VERO

Fondamenta Misericordia 2497
041 275 0044
[MAP p. 177 F3]

Vino Vero means Real Wine and this snug waterfront wine bar-cum-shop pours just that: organic and low-interventionist drops. Exposed brickwork, sculptural lighting and a blackboard feature-wall set a contemporary scene for its mostly Italian and Slovenian drops. That said, it's not unusual to find yourself quaffing something fabulously French, Spanish or Portuguese. You might even find yourself mulling over a lesser-known vino from Georgia. Scan the blackboard for the day's offerings by the glass or simply let the barkeep guide you. There's genuine passion and knowledge behind the marble counter and it has often steered me towards unexpected and exciting winemakers I'd never come across. Another option: buy a bottle off the shop shelf and savour it onsite (corkage fee applies). If you're hungry, seasonal, produce-driven cicheti (Venetian tapas) are on standby, from crostini (small open-faced sandwiches) laden with pistachio cream and mortadella to niche artisan cheeses that might include crosta fiorita, northern Italy's answer to brie.

POCKET TIP

Venice Kayak
(venicekayak.com) runs guided
tours of Venice's waterways,
including three-hour and
full-day kayaking adventures.
Tours depart from the island
of Certosa, accessible
from Cannaregio on the
4.2 vaporetto (ferry).

ƧAN POLO

From San Marco, the Ponte di Rialto (Rialto Bridge) arches over the Grand Canal and slides into bustling San Polo, the city's smallest sestiere (district). Despite its relatively compact size, its mish-mash of snug bars, medieval churches and produce-laden stalls pack a punch. At its eastern edge, top-tier chefs and fastidious nonne (grandmothers) make a morning beeline for the Mercato di Rialto (Rialto Market, see p. 40), casting razor-sharp eyes over a cornucopia of regional delicacies, from island-grown carciofi (artichokes) to Adriatic seppie (cuttlefish). The streets closest to the market are home to cult-status cicheti (Venetian tapas) bars like All'Arco (see p. 47), often tucked away but rarely short of gastronomes craving bite-sized morsels topped with the day's freshest market ingredients.

Culture vultures swoop upon the precinct's western edge, home to two extraordinary cultural assets: Gothic church Basilica dei Frari (see p. 38) and the neighbouring Scuola Grande di San Rocco (see p. 39). While the former claims Titian's most celebrated masterpiece, the latter delivers a stirring sweep of Tintoretto canvases. Tangled between market and masterpieces are the neighbourhood's labyrinthine calli (streets), packed tightly with workaday locals, selfie-snapping tourists and a battalion of shops stocking everything from clichéd souvenirs to coveted Venetian stationery at Legatoria Polliero Venezia (see p. 44), locally designed bags from Process Collettivo (see p. 42), and avant-garde jewellery at Ohmyblue (see p. 43) for style provocateurs.

→ View of the Grand Canal from San Tomà vaporetto stop

SIGHTS
1. Basilica dei Frari
2. Scuola Grande di San Rocco

SIGHTS & SHOPPING
3. Mercato di Rialto (Rialto Market)

SHOPPING
4. Process Collettivo
5. Ohmyblue
6. Legatoria Polliero Venezia

EATING & DRINKING
7. Ristorante Regina Sconta
8. All'Arco
9. Cantina Do Mori
10. Pasticceria Rizzardini

DRINKING
11. Il Mercante

1 BASILICA DEI FRARI

Campo dei Frari 3072
041 272 8618
[MAP p. 171 C2]

This 14th century behemoth is the Franciscans' answer to the Dominicans' Zanipolo (*see* p. 86). A vast, Gothic blockbuster, the church houses Titian's luminous *Assunta* (Assumption of the Virgin), the largest wood-panel painting in the world and the very painting that confirmed Titian's place in the pantheon of Renaissance greats. Although Titian himself was interred here in 1576, his Carrara-marble mausoleum (in the right nave) was only completed in 1852 by Luigi Zandomeneghi and his son Pietro. The commission had originally been awarded to neoclassical sculptor Antonio Canova in 1790, though dwindling funds and the collapse of the Venetian Republic soon halted plans. Canova's efforts weren't completely in vain: his own moving memorial (in the left nave) takes inspiration from the never-realised monument. Executed by five of Canova's students, and home to his actual heart, the pyramid-shaped work is rich in Masonic symbolism, a nod to Canova's Freemason ways.

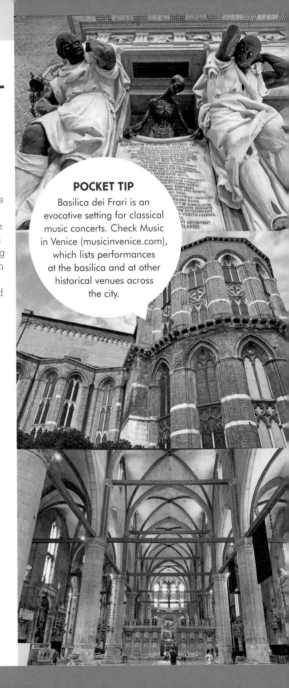

POCKET TIP
Basilica dei Frari is an evocative setting for classical music concerts. Check Music in Venice (musicinvenice.com), which lists performances at the basilica and at other historical venues across the city.

2 SCUOLA GRANDE DI SAN ROCCO

Campo San Rocco 3052
041 523 4864
[MAP p. 170 C4]

Tintoretto's brilliance reaches fever pitch at this 16th-century lay confraternity, wrapped in one of the most breathtaking painting cycles in the history of Venetian art. Start your visit chronologically in the upstairs Charter Hall, where Tintoretto's canvases turn walls and a gold-painted ceiling into veritable movie screens. Look up to catch famous moments from the Old Testament before musing on the life of Christ, whose backstory continues in the Ground Floor Hall. No doubt Tintoretto's contemporaries (among them Veronese) would still be cursing the artist from beyond the grave. Determined to secure the commission, Tintoretto shrugged off the official call for sketches, producing an actual painting of *St Roch in Glory* and installing it in the upstairs Sala dell'Albergo without permission. His prospective clients accepted the gift and granted Tintoretto the gig of a lifetime. Other treasures include Giorgione's superb painting *Christ Carrying the Cross*, crowned by a luminous lunette attributed to Titian and his team.

POCKET TIP

Some of Venice's greatest artists contributed to the nearby Scuola Grande di San Giovanni Evangelista (Campiello de la Scuola 2454), worth a visit for Giorgio Massari's lavish St John's Hall alone.

3 MERCATO DI RIALTO (RIALTO MARKET)

Campo de la Pescaria
[MAP p. 169 E2]

Venice's best-loved communal larder has been peddling produce for seven centuries. It's an appetite-piquing sight, as satisfying for photo ops and people watching as it is for stocking up your own kitchen rental in Venice. Aim and shoot at the season's finest edibles: springtime castraure (violet baby artichokes), early-summer fiori di zucca (zucchini flowers), woody porcini mushrooms in autumn, tangy radicchio trevisano (Treviso chicory) in winter. For the full effect, head in early in the morning (Saturdays are especially buzzing), when scrupulous locals are on the hunt for the day's prime offerings. Under neo-Gothic arches, fishmongers hawk their wares at the market's Pescaria, their own stalls loaded with vongole (clams), seppie (squid), moscardini (baby octopus) and silvery, bright-eyed pesci (fish). Shop sustainably by opting for locally caught critters, labelled 'nostrano'. The fruit and vegetable section of the market operates Monday to Saturday 7am to 8pm, while the Pescaria trades Tuesday to Saturday 7am to 2pm.

POCKET TIP

A market visit should include a stop at the Aliani family's Casa del Parmigiano (Campo Cesare Battisti già della Bella Vienna 214), a veteran deli stocking high-quality formaggi (cheeses), salumi (cured meats), wines and more.

4 PROCE//
COLLETTIVO

Fondamenta Frari 2559
041 524 3125
[MAP p. 171 C2]

Shop local and help a noble
cause at this not-for-profit
concept store. A collaboration
between US artist Mark
Bradford and Rio Terà dei
Pensieri – a local association
providing voluntary training
and employment to inmates
at Venetian prisons – it's
an awesome spot to snap
up contemporary Venetian-
designed clothes, accessories
and gifts. Top picks include
organic-cotton graphic
tees with playful Venetian
themes and striking PVC
totes, handbags and toiletry
bags made using upcycled
billboards. The small-batch,
unisex beauty products are
also good buys, made using
botanicals grown in the former
convent garden of the women's
prison in Giudecca. Best of
all, while the range – which
includes soaps, gels, scrubs,
haircare products, moisturisers,
fragrances and diffusers – is
good enough for luxe hotels
like the Bauer, prices are for
the mere-mortal.

POCKET TIP

Frescoed Palazzetto Bru Zane
(Campiello del Forner o del
Marangon 2368) hosts intimate
concerts of historic French music,
from chamber to operatic.
Guided tours of the building
run on Thursday afternoons
(bru-zane.com).

5 OHMYBLUE

Campo San Tomà 2865
041 243 5741
[MAP p. 171 C3]

Expect to OMG at OMB, a white-washed boutique-gallery dedicated to cutting-edge jewellery and couture. At the helm is the effortlessly stylish, affable Elena Rizzi, who curates the collections with sibling Chiaralice, an award-winning visual artist. Their selections are on-point and progressive, spotlighting some of the freshest design talent in Italy and beyond. Look out for jewellery by Berlin-based artist Denise Reytan, whose collage-like pieces combine materials as varied as silicone, plastic and precious gemstones for a pop-Baroque effect. You might also find wearable steel sculptures by Amsterdam-based talent Julia Walter or experimental rings made of glass, cubic zirconia and shakudo by Milan-based designer Federica Sala. While the collection of threads by renowned Japanese designers Yohji Yamamoto and Issey Miyake are arguably less 'independent', they're suitably out of the box, pushing boundaries with bold silhouettes, geometrics and fabrics.

6 LEGATORIA POLLIERO VENEZIA

Campo dei Frari 2995
041 528 5130
[MAP p. 171 C2]

Following in the footsteps of nonno Bruno and father Renato, renowned bookbinder Anselmo Pollieri makes stationery that will leave you itching to pick up a paintbrush or pen. Sketchbooks and journals are bound in Italian leather, the majority of them hand-sewn by the industrious hands of Anselmo's mother Paola. Smaller notebooks will set you back about €13, with 200-gram cotton-paper diaries and sketchpads retailing for around €25. Paper and leather are also put to fetching use in Anselmo's range of picture frames, while his printed paper is made using mostly late 19th-century Italian patterns. Some of it is actually printed using rare woodcuts from Pakistan and India, bought by Renato from an antiques dealer in the Dolomites. In a city where artisans are an increasingly threatened species, it's the sense of generational continuity that I especially love here, one that extends to some of the store's faithful, intergenerational customers.

7 RISTORANTE REGINA SCONTA

Calle Regina 2259a
041 524 3858
[MAP p. 168 C2]

Dressed in weathered bricks and patterned timber floors, this intimate, hidden highlight goes against the local grain, favouring turf over surf. Many of the meats hail from the fertile Friulian Alps, and most are free range and organic. Attention to detail underscores all the produce, which owner and chef Andrea Bovo transforms into cracking dishes that might include homemade gnocchetti (small gnocchi) served with duck ragù and blue cheese aged in Raboso (a red Veneto wine) or a sweet-and-sour quail millefoglie with celery-and-hazelnut pesto. In winter, find comfort in Andrea's bollito, a northern-Italian stew made using five cuts of boiled meat, seasonal vegetables and served with various sauces. Andrea's partner, Ylenia Gasparotto, runs front of house and her love of lesser-known Italian winemakers might see you quaffing exceptional vino from Fiegl, a sustainable producer the couple discovered on a Sunday drive along the Italian–Slovenian border. Phone ahead to book at least three days in advance for Friday or Saturday dinner, especially in winter.

8 ALL'ARCO

Calle de l'Ochialer 436
041 520 5666
[MAP p. 169 E3]

Ask a Venetian (or food-obsessed travel writer) to reel off their favourite cicheti bars and All'Arco will most likely top the list. Run by the jovial Francesco Pinto and his son Matteo, the tiny hotspot pulls peckish shoppers, local workers and lucky tourists, sipping quality ombre (small glasses of wine) and polishing off bite-sized morsels made using top-tier Mercato di Rialto (Rialto Market) produce (*see* p. 40). Head in before noon to avoid the inevitable lunchtime throng, when all and sundry lust over just-made crostini (small open-faced sandwiches) with combos like prosciutto, caramelised onions and freshly grated horseradish root or plump prawns with bottarga (cured fish roe). While crostini make up the majority of offerings, heartier, old-school dishes are sometimes offered, from moscardini in umido (baby octopus stew) to comforting zuppa di trippa (tripe soup). Note: like most bacari (wine bars), the place is standing-room only, with only a handful of tables outside.

POCKET TIP

Urban Adventures (urbanadventures.com) runs popular cicheti (Venetian tapas) and wine tours of Venice. Tours support locally owned and loved businesses.

9 CANTINA DO MORI

Calle Do Mori 429
041 522 5401
[MAP p. 169 E3]

A Rembrandt-esque scene of old copper pots and plates, wrought-iron lanterns and retro spumante glasses, 'Two Moors' feels like you're stepping into an Old Masters' painting. The place has been dabbling in vino since the 1460s, when monks from adjoining monasteries used the space to turn grapes into wine. More than half a millennium later, it's one of the city's best bacari (wine bars). Regardless of whether you're local or a traveller, staff cheerfully guide the lost and indecisive through the plethora of cicheti (Venetian tapas). Personal favourites here include succulent zucchini polpette (meatballs), artichoke hearts, regional ubriaco (prosecco-infused cheese) and hard-boiled eggs topped with salty anchovies. A generous list of pan-Italian wines by the glass cover all budgets, from easy drinking €3 and €4 pours of Friulano, Lugana, Lagrein and Etna Rosso, to €13 and €15 offerings of blockbuster Amarone, Barolo and Brunello rarely offered by the glass.

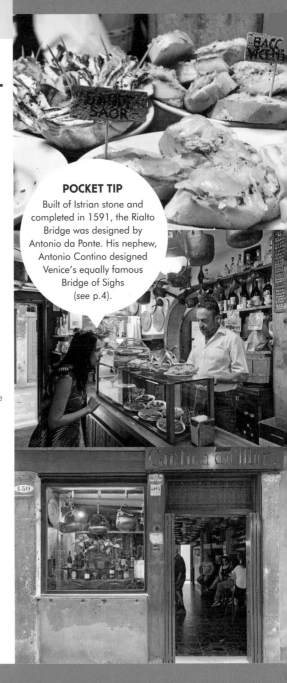

POCKET TIP

Built of Istrian stone and completed in 1591, the Rialto Bridge was designed by Antonio da Ponte. His nephew, Antonio Contino designed Venice's equally famous Bridge of Sighs (see p.4).

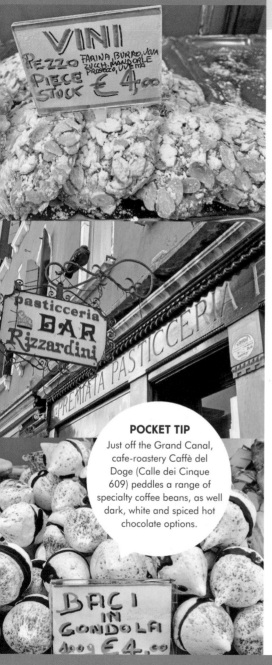

10 PASTICCERIA RIZZARDINI

Campiello dei Meloni 1415
041 522 3835
[MAP p. 168 C4]

Rizzardini has been enabling love handles since 1742. While the carved walnut shelves are an early 20th-century addition, little else has changed here since. Windows and counters are lined with traditional sweets: sticky, nutty croccanti; prosecco-infused vini; and succulent, chocolatey strudel Venezia. Regulars drop in like clockwork, punctuating sips of espresso or orzo (a hot barley drink) with sing-song Venetian chit-chat. The coffee is strong, good and made with locally roasted beans from neighbouring Caffè del Doge. Standout edibles include the zurigo (apple puff pastry) and fiamma éclair, the latter filled with impossibly light zabaione (marsala-infused cream). Come Easter or Christmas, order their sweet, fragrant focaccia, a lighter local version of Milan's yeasty panettone cake. On your way out, note the flood-level marker by the entrance, a record of historic acque alte (tidal floods).

POCKET TIP

Just off the Grand Canal, cafe-roastery Caffè del Doge (Calle dei Cinque 609) peddles a range of specialty coffee beans, as well dark, white and spiced hot chocolate options.

49

11 IL MERCANTE

Fondamenta Frari 2564
347 829 3158
[MAP p. 171 C2]

As evening descends, Caffè dei Frari pulls out its jigger and moonlights as Il Mercante, one of Venice's more serious cocktail bars. Its genial drinks list is based on rotating themes, from literature to global cuisines. Cocktails are paired with specific snacks, specially created to complement each drink's flavour profile. This might mean a gin-based libation of artichoke, elderflower, pink grapefruit and St Germaine paired with herbs and flower jellies, or an Amatriciana-inspired blend of vodka, dry vermouth and black tea coupled with parmesan foam, pineapple gel and balsamic vinegar. Not that this historic space is new to subversion. It was once a brothel, its working ladies showing off their wares from the elliptical balcony above. As for the framed felines adoring the stairwell, they're an ode to Nini, a neighbourhood cat so aristocratic that even the Tzar of Russia reputedly stopped by for a meet, greet and pat.

ſANTA CROCE

On first impressions, Santa Croce can feel like an imposter. Connected to the mainland via the Ponte della Libertà, this is the city's service entry. Taxis, trams and buses stream into Piazzale Roma, transporting endless streams of tourists and commuters. Motorists navigate multi-story carparks, while further west, cruise ships unleash the day-tripping hordes, sightseeing checklists at the ready. Add a splattering of mediocre modern buildings and the district resembles the ill-fitting piece of a Venetian jigsaw. But while there's no denying the aesthetic shortcomings of Santa Croce's western half, wander further east and you'll discover a very different Santa Croce.

In this other half, sleepy canals, medieval streets and workaday campi (squares) lay on the charm with their crumbly façades, idiosyncratic shops and authentic, low-key vibe. Not that the neighbourhood is all strung laundry, dusty hardware stores and dirt-cheap bacari (wine bars). Exceptional locavore restaurants like Osteria Trefanti (see p. 60) draw clued-in gastronomes while on (and just off) the Grand Canal, the frescoed palaces of Venetian nobility harbour cultural treasures, from daring modern masterpieces and maverick glassware at Ca' Pesaro (see p. 54) to rare historical fashion at nearby Palazzo Mocenigo (see p. 55).

→ *Early morning light washing over Rio Marin*

SIGHTS
1. Ca' Pesaro
2. Museo di Palazzo Mocenigo

SHOPPING
3. Il Grifone
4. Paperoowl

EATING & DRINKING
5. Osteria La Zucca
6. Osteria da Filo
7. Osteria Trefanti
8. Bacareto da Lele

1 CA' PESARO

Fondamenta de Ca' Pesaro 2076
041 72 11 27
[MAP p. 168 C1]

When Madonna-and-Child overload hits, Ca' Pesaro is your detox. Designed by Baroque architect Baldassare Longhena and finished by Gian Antonio Gaspari after Longhena's death in 1682, the frescoed former pad of the noble Pesaro family houses both the **Galleria d'Arte Moderna** and the **Museo d'Arte Orientale**. The former claims Venice's top collection of modern and contemporary art, showcasing artists as diverse as Rodin, Chagall, Kandinsky, Lichtenstein and Koons. Seek out Gustav Klimt's celebrated *Judith II*, Giorgio de Chirico's *The Night of Pericles* and *Mysterious Baths*, and Mario Sironi's dystopian *Urban Landscape*. The collection of superb glassware includes pieces by 20th-century Venetian architect Carlo Scarpa. One floor up is the underrated Museo d'Arte Orientale, a creaky attic of Asian artefacts that include Edo-period weaponry, lacquerware and silk paintings, as well as Islamic ceramics spanning numerous centuries.

POCKET TIP

Venezia Unica City Pass (veneziaunica.it) covers 11 civic museums, including Palazzo Ducale (see p. 4) and Museo Correr (see p. 6). The tourist card can be customised to also include city transport and wi-fi.

2 MUSEO DI PALAZZO MOCENIGO

Salizada San Stae 1992
041 72 17 98
[MAP p. 168 B1]

Real-estate envy is inevitable at this sumptuous waterfront palace. From the 17th to mid-20th-centuries, it was home to the San Stae branch of the Mocenigo family, of whom seven members became doges between 1414 and 1778. While the VIPs may have moved out, the artworks and sumptuous interiors remain, offering a glimpse of gilded Venetian life as it once was. Among these are a series of late 18th-century ceiling frescoes – executed by Jacopo Guarana, Giambattista Canal and Giovanni Scajar to celebrate the wedding of Doge Alvise IV's grandson – as well as large-scale canvases depicting pomp and pageantry. What really makes the place special, however, is its cachet of exquisite 18th-century fashions, among them embroidered gowns, capes and tailcoats. The museum also includes an interactive section exploring fragrance; a suitable subject given Venice's former role as a European capital of perfume production.

3 IL GRIFONE

Fondamenta del Gaffaro 3516
041 522 9452
[MAP p. 170 A4]

Self-taught, softly spoken Antonio (aka Tony) opened his leather workshop in 1985. Decades later, he's still here. With son Filippo, the bearded maestro carves, lines and stitches coveted leather products in the crammed room behind the counter. There's no hype, no sales push and no faux flattery here. Just simple, stylish, handcrafted products in hues ranging from classic and restrained, to bright and bold. Only vegetable-tanned leather from Tuscany and Veneto is used, shaped into items ranging from butter-soft women's handbags, to coin purses and trays, streamlined wallets, belts and toiletry bags. Quality is high and prices palatable: expect to pay around €13 for a keyring, €55 for a wallet, €85 for a laptop sleeve or around €145 for a handbag. While it's hard not to find something to fawn over, custom pieces are also available, usually taking a few weeks to make. International shipping is available.

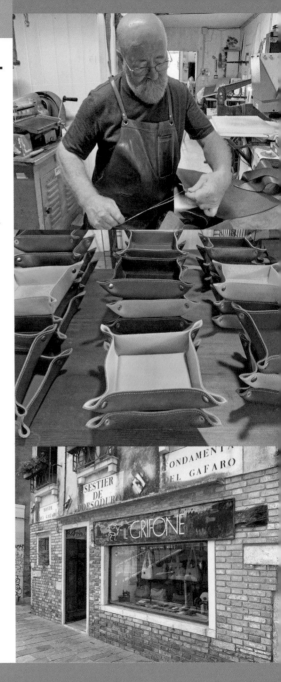

4 PAPEROOWL

Calle Longa 2155a
041 476 1974
[MAP p. 168 B2]

In 2012, Stefania Giannici took a chance and entered the Lucca Biennale, one of the world's most prestigious paper-art competitions. She ended up a finalist: not bad for someone with no formal art training. Today, you'll find the Verona native in her tranquil studio, transforming paper into remarkable creations. Small, stripy boxes slide open to reveal dioramas of Venetian scenes and palazzi, from Gothic landmarks like Ca' Pesaro and Ca' d'Oro, to modern icons like the Palazzo del Cinema di Venezia. A knack for origami shines through in her intricate kuzudama flower balls (traditionally used to ward off evil spirits), while some of the paper earrings are decorated with gold leaf from the only gold-beating workshop left in Venice, Mario Berta Battiloro. Note that opening times can vary, so consider calling ahead if making a special trip.

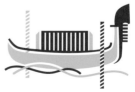

5 OSTERIA LA ZUCCA

Calle del Tentor 1762
041 524 1570
[MAP p. 168 A1]

In Italian, La Zucca means 'the pumpkin', which is an apt name given that this Slow-Food bastion champions vegetables in all their seasonal glory. While not technically a vegetarian eatery, herbivores won't go hungry, which is just as well given that the food here is honest, flavourful and a change from the standard Venetian repertoire. Market-driven dishes run from sweet, succulent figs stuffed with herbed caprino (goat's cheese) to fluffy pumpkin flan with sage butter and smoked ricotta. Global influences also scatter the menu – think calvados duck breast, coconut curry chicken or a side of Eastern-spiced lentils with tzatziki – while dessert balances classic tiramisu with surprises like passionfruit aspic jelly with caramelised pineapple. It's good, solid comfort food with a retro accent, suitably served in an oak-planked 1980s flashback slung with original sketches and watercolours. Space is limited so make reservations a few days ahead online (lazucca.it), especially if you're after one of the coveted alfresco tables.

6 OSTERIA DA FILO

Calle del Tentor 1539
041 524 6554
[MAP p. 168 A2]

Cheap, quaffable drinks, tasty cicheti (Venetian tapas) and an arty, come-one-come-all vibe make 'La Poppa' a must for a neighbourly tipple. Each night, regulars spill out onto the street, clutching craft IPAs and organic Verdicchios, scoffing polpette (meatballs), cheeses and cured meats, and chatting about uni exams, politics and music. The place itself feels like a communal living room, packed with mismatched furniture, op-shop mirrors, old books, glowing lamps and chilled barkeeps bantering with the steady stream of familiar faces. Venetians outweigh the Tripadvisor brigade, making it one of the best spots to fake it as a local. If you're into live tunes, drop in on a Wednesday, when homegrown or visiting acts usually serve up jazz or blues. Check da Filo's Facebook page for upcoming events.

7 OJTERIA TREFANTI

Fondamenta del Rio Marin o
dei Garzoti 888
041 520 1789
[MAP p. 170 C2]

When Venice-bound friends
ask me for restaurant
recommendations, intimate
Osteria Trefanti *always* makes
the cut. Elegantly simple and
light-filled, its attention to
detail is impeccable, from the
music and stemware, to the
printed paper bags filled with
beautiful breads. For owner
and chef Umberto Slongo,
Osteria Trefanti is a love letter
to his city, its history and
geography. Seafood is the
main protagonist, with the
intermittent use of spices a
nod to Venice's spice-trading
past. The menu is short and
variable, dictated by first-rate
market produce and farm
deliveries. The result: polished,
nuanced dishes which might
see succulent gamberoni (large
prawns) served with summer
berries and paprika for subtle
smokiness, or seabass ravioli
paired with delicate zucchini
and saffron threads. Leave room
for dessert, which features
cakes baked by Umberto's
mother, Luisa. Thoughtfulness
also drives the wine list, where
the odd Greek or Georgian drop
also pays homage to Venice's
cosmopolitan pedigree.
Book ahead.

POCKET TIP

Tradition and innovation make for fine bed fellows at Zanze XVI (Santa Croce 231, zanze.it), one of Venice's more forward-thinking restaurants. Reservations are always a good idea, especially later in the week.

61

8 BACARETO DA LELE

Campo dei Tolentini 183
[MAP p. 170 A4]

From dawn to dusk, old-timers, office workers and euro-pinching students from the nearby Università Iuav di Venezia squeeze into this cupboard of a bacaro (wine bar) for dirt-cheap ombre (small glasses of wine) and paninetti (small sandwiches). The day's vino – anything from cabernet and raboso to chardonnay and glera – are listed on a blackboard and poured for as little at €0.70. Behind the tiny counter, good-humoured staffers pump out an endless stream of fresh, crusty mini sandwiches. Fillings are varied and mouthwatering, ranging from mortadella, prosciutto, pancetta and speck, to marinated vegetables and luscious slices of formaggio (cheese). Wine and edibles in hand, squeeze your way out to devour them at a wine-barrel table or by the canal. If you're anything like me, you'll quickly end up back in the queue, ready for round two. Note that the bar is closed for much of August.

POCKET TIP

Grab a gelato from Gelato di Natura (Calle Larga 1627) and chill in leafy Campo San Giacomo da l'Orio. The square is home to the 13th-century Chiesa di San Giacomo dall'Orio.

DORSODURO

Lapped by the Grand and Giudecca canals, and with Basilica di Santa Maria della Salute (*see* p. 70) as its Baroque bow, Dorsoduro epitomises Venetian dolce vita. This is the Venice of affluent expats and their canalside palazzi, of prime-time art collections and jovial campi (squares) filled with late-night revellers. Its western end is awash with masterpieces, from epic Renaissance canvases at the Gallerie dell'Accademia (*see* p. 66) to Chandler, Moore and Pollock in the unfinished pad of free-thinking Peggy Guggenheim (*see* p. 68). Canaletto, Tiepolo and Pietro Longhi's satirical brushstrokes await in the frescoed rooms of Ca' Rezzonico (*see* p. 68), the Grand Canal palace in which English poet Robert Browning met his maker. Further east, refined contemplation gives way to raucous bonhomie in sun-soaked Campo San Margherita, eternal hotspot of spritz-sipping, beer-swilling students and all-round pleasure seekers.

Sandwiched in between them all are Dorsoduro's narrow calli (streets) and canals, punctuated by neighbourly osterie (taverns), erudite bookshops, artisan workshops and curated boutiques. You'll find glassware, antiques, art and artisan masks in Calle delle Botteghe; fashion, design, rare books and prints on Calle Lunga San Barnaba; and locally frequented cicheti (Venetian tapas) bars on canalside Fondamenta Nani. At its southern end, Fondamenta Nani hits Fondamenta delle Zattere, a luminous esplanade where cocktails and gelato are served with sweeping views across to the island of Giudecca.

↤ *Canal-side chilling at Malvasia all'Adriatico Mar*

SIGHTS
1. Gallerie dell'Accademia
2. Peggy Guggenheim Collection
3. Basilica di Santa Maria della Salute

SHOPPING
4. Libreria MarcoPolo
5. Enogastronomia Pantagruelica
6. Paolo Olbi
7. Marisa Convento at Bottega Cini

EATING & DRINKING
8. Estro
9. Cantine del Vino già Schiavi
10. Pasticceria Tonolo
11. Malvasia all'Adriatico Mar
12. El Sbarlefo

1 GALLERIE DELL'ACCADEMIA

Campo de la Carità 1050
041 524 3354
[MAP p. 172 C2]

Home to the world's largest collection of Venetian art, the Accademia's hallowed halls – some revamped by architect Carlo Scarpa – celebrate the brightest stars of the 14th to 19th centuries. It's a veritable crash course in the city's artistic evolution, worthy of an entire morning or afternoon and littered with celebrated masterpieces from Bellini, Titian, Tintoretto, Veronese and Canaletto. Among these is Veronese's *The Feast in the House of Levi* – the depiction of boozed-up, bawdy characters drew unfavourable attention during the Roman Inquisition of the 16th century. Keep an eye out for Gentile Bellini's *Procession in Piazza San Marco*, especially fascinating for its depiction of the famed square before its 16th-century makeover. Temporary exhibitions include the occasional contemporary artist, though it's the permanent collection that really shines. As is to be expected, the museum draws big crowds in high season, so turn up right on opening time or spend the extra €1.50 to purchase your ticket online (gallerieaccademia.it).

POCKET TIP

State-run museums, including the Gallerie dell'Accademia, are free on the first Sunday of the month. The downside: larger crowds. Google 'Musei statali di Venezia' for a full list.

2 PEGGY GUGGENHEIM COLLECTION

Calle San Cristoforo 701
041 240 5411
[MAP p. 173 B4]

American heiress Peggy Guggenheim was a one-woman cultural powerhouse, amassing an extraordinary cachet of avant-garde 20th-century art: Braque, Chagall, Dalí, Duchamp, Kadinsky, Klee, Magritte, Miró, Mondrian, Moore, Picasso, Pollock, Rothko and so on. Peggy's second husband, Max Ernst, is in the inventory, alongside Italian Futurist Gino Severini, metaphysical pioneer Giorgio de Chirico, Venetian-born Emilio Vedova and sculptor Mario Marini. The latter created *The Angel of the City*, a cheeky, jubilant bronze nodding to Guggenheim's well-known love of culture and sex. The gallery – which incorporates the permanent collection, temporary exhibitions and sculpture garden (Peggy's final resting place) – occupies 18th-century Palazzo Venier dei Leoni, the unfinished Grand Canal palace the collector called home from 1949 until her death in 1979. Some of her famous friends contributed to the palace décor; you'll find Alexander Calder's Silver Bedhead (1946) in the former bedroom.

POCKET TIP
Grand Canal palace Ca' Rezzonico (Fondamenta Rezzonico 3136) is a cultural treasure trove, its drawcards including Tiepolo frescoes, Canaletto's *View of Venice* and Pietro Longhi's tongue-in-cheek depictions of 18th-century life.

3 BASILICA DI SANTA MARIA DELLA SALUTE

Campo de la Salute 1
[MAP p. 173 C4]

Not all gifts are created equal.
Take Baldassare Longhena's
wedding-cake basilica, the
Venetian Senate's 'grazie'
(thank you) to the Madonna
for delivering Venice from
the devastating plague
of 1630. A commanding
concoction of Istrian stone,
it's one of Venice's most iconic
landmarks, not to mention a
suitably grand bookend to the
Grand Canal. It's also one of its
most mystical. The building's
octagonal shape echoes Jewish
Kabbalah diagrams, while
the black dot at the centre
of the vortex below the central
dome is said to emit healing
energy. The vortex itself is
a spectacular example of
marble inlay, set dramatically
against elegantly restrained
arches and balustrades. Fans
of 16th-century master Titian
will find several of his artworks
here, including his *Descent of
the Holy Spirit*, slung in a side
chapel near the entrance to the
sacristy. The latter – accessible
for a small fee – harbours
other works by Titian, as well
Tintoretto's appetite-piquing
Wedding Feast of Cana (that's
Tintoretto sitting at the
bottom-left corner in amber
robes and a beard).

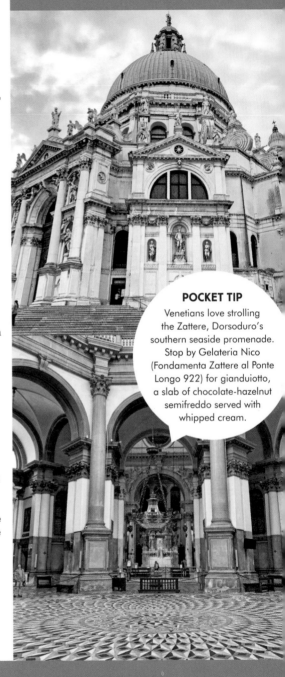

POCKET TIP
Venetians love strolling
the Zattere, Dorsoduro's
southern seaside promenade.
Stop by Gelateria Nico
(Fondamenta Zattere al Ponte
Longo 922) for gianduiotto,
a slab of chocolate-hazelnut
semifreddo served with
whipped cream.

4 LIBRERIA MARCOPOLO

Campo Santa Margherita 2899
041 822 4843
[MAP p. 172 B1]

Discerning Venetian bibliophiles feed their minds at this exemplary bookstore, which represents around 50 independent publishers. Owners Flavio, Claudio and Sabina have read almost every title on the shelves, and much of the stock is determined by what they've personally enjoyed reading. This includes titles in the thoughtfully curated English-language section, where you're bound to find anything from literary guides to Venice, to paperbacks from authors like Italo Calvino, Kate Clifford Larson and young Italian literary heavyweight Paolo Cognetti. English-language picture books on Venice are available in the dedicated children's room, while those after cool mementos will find Venice-themed graphic posters by local artist Anna Fietta. Look out for the bookstore's tote bag, which wisely proclaims: 'Don't look for love. Look for books'. Outside summer and December, the store usually hosts regular readings, talks and special events (check the website: libreriamarcopolo.com).

POCKET TIP

There's a second branch of Libreria MarcoPolo in Giudecca (Fondamenta Ponte Picolo 282), overlooking the Giudecca Canal and Venice skyline.

71

5
ENOGA/TRONOMIA PANTAGRUELICA

Campo San Barnaba
041 523 6766
[MAP p. 172 B1]

If you've rented an apartment, your pantry is probably pining for this Slow-Food deli. One of the best in the lagoon, it celebrates small producers and organic goods, from Italian wines and spirits, to cured meats, cheeses and pasta. It's a fantastic spot to bag niche comestibles, whether it be aged Parmigiano Reggiano made with the milk of prized vacche rosse (red cows), bresaola (air-dried, salted beef) made using Piedmontese Fassone, jars of Trapanese pesto or bottles of organic Brunello. Maurizio Gasparello – who runs the deli with his childhood sweetheart Silvia – is never short of anecdotes about the products and their makers, and I've spent many an enlightened visit learning about edibles I've never seen before. What makes this place extra special is that you can graze onsite, the couple serve a rotating selection of wines and artful taglieri (platters) laden with top-shelf salumi (cured meats), cheeses, olives and wood-fired bread (around €25 for two).

6 PAOLO OLBI

Calle Foscari 3253
041 523 7655
[MAP p. 171 B4]

Octogenarian Paolo Olbi is one of Venice's most respected bookbinders and papermakers, crafting hand-printed, hand-bound notebooks, sketchbooks, diaries and albums for over half a century. Far from your run-of-the-mill stationery, his creations are life-long keepsakes, made using traditional techniques that continue Venice's long illustrious history of papermaking, printing and bookbinding. Among these is carta marmorata (paper marbling), a technique producing strikingly patterned, marble-like paper, and embossed leather-binding. Prices span all budgets, with a number of smaller paperback notebooks and diaries offered for €25 or less. You'll even find postcards and bookmarks printed with fetching watercolour scenes of Venice that make bargain souvenirs. If he's not busy, politely ask to see signore Olbi's libro degli ospiti (guestbook), scribbled with a few famous names, among them the odd Hollywood hunk and a popular New York City mayor. While the store is officially closed on weekends, chances are you might find it open.

7 MARISA CONVENTO AT BOTTEGA CINI

Campo San Vio 862
370 3622439
[MAP p. 173 A4]

Resident artisan at concept store Bottega Cini, Marisa Convento is Venice's last impiraressa (bead stringer), threading tiny conterie (glass beads) to create beautiful bijoux and ornaments. Until the first half of the 20th century, impiraresse were a common sight on Venetian streets, many of them working-class women supporting husbands, fathers or brothers working at the Arsenale shipyards. Fascinated by the dying craft, Marisa Convento delved into its past, learning the techniques and bringing the tradition back to life. Only vintage Venetian beads are used and much of the work is custom made, taking anything from a few days to a few months to complete. These include Marisa's celebrated coralli, coral-shaped pieces used to decorate everything from necklines to bags, slippers and shoes. That said, ready-made options are available, among them fetching earrings for under €20.

8 E∫TRO

Calle Crosera 3778
041 476 4914
[MAP p. 171 B3]

Brothers Alberto and Dario
Spezzamonte helm this
polished enoteca and bistro.
The front bar is handy for a
quick vino and chiacchiera
(chat). Wines by the glass
change weekly, with around
15 to 18 offerings on the
blackboard on any given day.
There's usually a few more
off-menu, so consider asking
what else might be available
alla mescita (by the glass).
Dario takes care of the wines,
with over 700 bottled options,
all of them natural. While
Italian wines rightfully take
centre stage, you'll find some
unexpected foreign surprises.
On my last visit, the boys
pulled out a Mourvedre-Shiraz
blend from South Australia's
Barossa Valley. This open-
minded approach extends to
the back-room bistro, where
Alberto's modern, market-fresh
options might see you noshing
on house-smoked mackerel
parmigiana or calamarata
pasta, piovra (squid) and
chanterelle mushrooms served
with a scampi bisque. Grazers
can opt for an antipasto board
of charcuterie and house-
pickled nibbles.

9 CANTINE DEL VINO GIÀ /CHIAVI

Fondamenta Nani 992
041 523 0034
[MAP p. 172 C2]

If you *must* Instagram your cicheti (Venetian tapas), worthy subjects await at this cult-status tavern and wine shop, dressed head-to-toe in gleaming bottles of vino. The counter is a veritable cornucopia of creative and less-ubiquitous crostini (small open-faced sandwiches) toppings. Should you try the fluffy ricotta with pumpkin and grated parmigiano, the delicate octopus and celery, or the sheep's milk primosale cheese with spicy radicchio and sesame? Then again, the salmon and mascarpone looks good, as do the smoked herring, hazelnut mousse and combo of prawns, artichokes and truffle. You can blame septuagenarian owner Alessandra De Respinis for the conundrum, a woman who gets a kick from concocting new, unexpected morsels for her mix of faithful Venetians and clued-in out-of-towners. Whichever crostini you choose, wash them down with one of about 25 wines on offer, most of them hailing from Veneto vines.

10 PASTICCERIA TONOLO

Calle San Pantalon 3764
041 523 7209
[MAP p. 171 B3]

Mention Tonolo to Venetians and watch them drool discreetly. Trading since 1886, it's one of Venice's best-loved pasticcerie (pastry shops), where decent espresso is served in dainty porcelain cups and the daily tide of customers range from bawdy gondoliers to the odd traitorous Austrian stocking up on Sacher torte before the train ride home. Come Carnevale, peeps flock here for the city's best frittelle (fried dougnuts), offered in numerous varieties. My favourite is frittelle con zabaione, filled with a deceptively light Marsala cream. Zabaione also fills year-round hits bignè al zabaione (zabaione filled profiteroles) and fiamma al zabaione (zabaione-cream éclair), with other favourites including the tiramisu and apfelstrudel (apple-strudel pastry). Curiously, many Venetians prefer dry sweets over creamy ones and Tonolo's bags of Venetian biscotti – among them cornflour and raisin zaleti – make for practical and tasty take-home treats.

POCKET TIP
Nearby, at the northern end of Campo Santa Margherita, Calle de la Chiesa leads to a bridge from which you can view a canal-side mural by British street artist Banksy.

11 MALVASIA ALL'ADRIATICO MAR

Calle Crosera 3771
041 476 4322
[MAP p. 171 A3]

Natural wines and craft beers, personable service and a tiny wooden jetty for waterside sipping: snug Malvasia has all the right ingredients for a blissful break. The muse here is the Adriatic Sea, with both libations and nibbles preferencing the lands surrounding its blue expanse. Scan the blackboard and you might find a spritely pinot bianco from Bolzano or a bold Roditis from the Peloponnese, all sourced from winemakers that owners Francesco and Sira deal with directly. Limited food offerings are no less tied to terroir, whether it's a summery salad of Asiago cheese with fresh peaches or a surprisingly light frico, a cheese-and-potato pancake from the Friuli Venezia Giulia region. Graze-friendly cicheti (Venetian tapas), cheeses and charcuterie pique appetites at the marble-top counter, the latter ranging from cured pork sausage from Trentino to rustic salamis Francesco and Sira might discover on road trips.

12 EL SBARLEFO

Calle San Pantalon 3757
041 524 6650
[MAP p. 171 B3]

Italian architecture buffs will appreciate this skinny bar, a loving homage to 20th-century Venetian architect Carlo Scarpa (right down to the replica Olivetti showroom floor). Design specs aside, the place pulls regulars with its house-infused gins and variations on the spritz. Among these is a proper classic spritz, made using still white wine, not prosecco. Cocktails are well mixed and the well-priced wines by the glass include the odd luxe Amarone or Barolo. When peckish, I ask for an assaggio (tasting plate) of the bar bites on display, which range from olive ascolane (stuffed fried olives) and mozzarella-stuffed zucchini flowers, to mildly spicy moscardini (baby octopus) served crostino style (as a small open-faced sandwich). If you're wondering about the piano in the back room, the place hosts live blues, jazz, bossa nova or rock, usually two Fridays a month from October to May.

POCKET TIP

Popular drinking spots on nearby Campo Santa Margherita include tiny Ai Do Draghi (3665) and historic Caffè Rosso (2963). For cheap, late-night munchies, hit Pizza Al Volo (2944).

CASTELLO

Its weathered streets festooned with freshly washed laundry, earthy Castello remains the most authentic of Venetian sestieri (districts). Here, shops still peddle pet supplies, haberdashery and bathroom fittings, Venetian dialect is thick in the air, and old-school bars entertain feverish debates about politics and Venezia FC. Mixed among them is a string of artisan studios and galleries, selling everything from handmade leather goods and city-themed watercolours, to homoerotic plates.

Castello's history is indelibly tied to its crenelated Arsenale (*see* p. 84), once the largest naval dockyard in medieval Europe, it's now best known for hosting the city's world-famous biennales of art and architecture. It's a role it shares with the Giardini della Biennale (Biennale Gardens, see p. 87), a swathe of green commissioned by Napoleon in 1807. Flanking the neighbourhood's southern edge is the Riva dei Sette Martiri (and its extension, the Riva degli Schiavoni), which shoots north-west towards Piazza San Marco in one spectacular, uninterrupted panorama of architectural landmarks.

The largest of Venice's historic districts, Castello also claims some of La Serenissima's most underrated cultural assets. Among these is the gloriously Gothic Basilica dei SS Giovanni e Paolo (aka: San Zanipolo, *see* p. 86), eternal resting place of many a Venetian ruler.

→ *Plants for sale at Serra dei Giardini*

SIGHTS
1. Arsenale
2. Basilica dei SS Giovanni e Paolo (San Zanipolo)
3. Giardini della Biennale (Biennale Gardens)

SIGHTS & SHOPPING
4. Paolo Brandolisio

SHOPPING
5. Banco Lotto N.10
6. Atelier Alessandro Merlin
7. Kalimala
8. Ceramiche Chimera
9. Libreria Acqua Alta

EATING & DRINKING
10. Nevodi
11. Gibran
12. Salvmeria
13. In Paradiso
14. Al Covo

1 AR/ENALE

Campo de l'Arsenal
[MAP p. 165 F3]

A symbol of the military
and mercantile muscle of
the Venetian Republic, this
sprawling ship-building
complex was founded in
1104. Reaching its zenith
between the 15th and 17th
centuries, its use of canals as
moving assembly lines made
the Arsenale a prototype
for modern manufacturing.
It was an impressive feat,
its 16,000-plus workforce
churning out one ready-to-
use warship every few hours.
During the Venice Biennale,
you can access its Artiglierie
(artillery workshop), Corderia
(cable-making workshop) and
arcaded Gaggiandre (dry dock),
designed by Renaissance
architect Jacopo Sansovino.
The only section open year-
round is the mid-16th-century
Padiglione delle Navi
(Fondamenta de la Tana 2126),
a timber-beamed warehouse
filled with an eclectic
assortment of historical
vessels. The Padiglione is an
annex of the nearby, take-it-
or-leave-it **Museo Storico
Navale** (Riva San Biagio 2148).
Beside the Padiglione is the
Arsenale's mid-15th-century
Porta Magna, a twin-towered
gate known as one of Venice's
earliest Renaissance structures.

POCKET TIP

For an easy escape in the summer, catch a vaporetto (ferry) from the Arsenale stop to Lido di Venezia, a sinuous, suburban island known for its sandy beaches, lively bars and faded glamour.

2 BAſILICA DEI ſſ GIOVANNI E PAOLO (ſAN ZANIPOLO)

Campo SS Giovanni e Paolo
041 523 5913
[MAP p. 167 D2]

When you're the final resting place of 25 Venetian doges, you're clearly no run-of-the-mill church. Built between 1333 and the 1430s, this Italian–Gothic behemoth hosted ducal funerals from the 15th century onward. Contrary to popular belief, the basilica's namesakes are not the famous apostles John and Paul, but two little-known soldier–martyr saints. Both make a cameo in the south transept's stained-glass window, standing beside St George and St Theodore, two of Venice's three patron saints. Crafted in Murano, the window itself is a rare example of 15th-century stained glass. Take time to also appreciate the ducal tombs, especially the three-tiered tomb of Doge Pietro Mocenigo, designed by Renaissance architect Pietro Lombardo. The basilica's high altar is attributed to Baroque high achiever Baldassare Longhena, best known for his Basilica di Santa Maria della Salute (*see* p. 70) on the Grand Canal. Another Venetian great, Paolo Veronese, awaits you on the ceiling of the Cappella del Rosario.

3 GIARDINI DELLA BIENNALE (BIENNALE GARDENS)

Calle Giazzo
041 521 8711
[MAP p. 182 C3]

You can thank Napoleon for commissioning Venice's precious green lungs. Designed by Venetian neoclassical architect Giannantonio Selva and opened in 1812, the 43,000-square-metre (450,000-square-foot) swathe of green is one of two major venues that host the city's esteemed art and architecture Biennales (the other being the Arsenale, *see* p. 84). Artists are exhibited in an eclectic collection of pavilions designed by prolific world architects like Josef Hoffman (Austrian Pavilion; 1934), Alvar Aalto (Finnish Pavilion; 1956) and Sverre Fehn (Nordic Pavilion; 1962). I find the latter especially beautiful, its clean, crisp lines encapsulating the very essence of Scandinavia. Pay tribute to the city's late great modernist Carlo Scarpa by contemplating the beautiful textures and detailing of the concrete Venezuelan Pavilion (1954), as well as the clever play of light and shade in his Central Pavilion Sculpture Garden (1952).

4 PAOLO BRANDOLISIO

Sotoportego Corte Rota 4725
041 522 4155
[MAP p. 164 A2]

Paolo Brandolisio is a Venetian rarity: one of only a handful of reméri (oar-and-oarlock craftsmen) left in town. The artisan was once the protégé of master remér Giuseppe Carli, whose handcrafted gondola fórcole (oarlocks) made their way into New York's Museum of Modern Art. Paolo inherited both the ancient craft and Giuseppe's dusty workshop, hidden off a razor-thin Castello street. In a city threatened by mass tourism and rampant commercialism, watching Paolo at work is both comforting and a privilege. In here, past and present are one and Venice's soul looms large. It takes Paolo eight to 10 hours to craft an oar and three days to sculpt an oarlock, each of which is customised for its gondolier. And while you may not need an oarlock yourself, Paolo's miniature replicas make for unique Venetian sculptures. As for the leftover timber, it's upcycled to make creatively shaped chopping blocks which are also for sale.

5 BANCO LOTTO N.10

Salizada Sant'Antonin 3478a
041 522 1439
[MAP p. 165 D2]

Everything on the racks at Banco Lotto N.10 is made by inmates at Giudecca's women's prison. It's part of a retraining programme, teaching incarcerated women sartorial skills and paying them for their labour. While the social aspect is reason enough to support the cause, the hand-cut threads impress in their own right. Beautiful tailoring and high-quality fabrics (including the odd roll from prestigious Venetian textile houses like Rubelli and Bevilacqua) underscore everything from '50s-inspired swing dresses to silk jackets and velvet capes. Pieces are either limited or one-offs, and most can be altered slightly on request; tweaks take between three days and two weeks. Expect to pay between €130 and €180 for a cotton frock or around €200 for a silk dress. Accessories include silk purse pouches, headbands and fabric brooches, all under €25. All in all, it's a fabulous fate for what was once a mid-century betting shop, now offering grounded hope in the form of fashion.

POCKET TIP

Gothic Chiesa di San Giovanni in Bragora (Campo Bandiera e Moro) houses the red-marble font used to baptise composer Antonio Vivaldi. Across the square lies historic coffee roaster Caffè Girani.

6 ATELIER ALE//ANDRO MERLIN

Calle del Pestrin 3876
041 522 5895
[MAP p. 165 E2]

Fire Jean Cocteau, Pablo Picasso and Tom of Finland together in a kiln and you'd end up with Alessandro Merlin's ceramics. His gleaming plates, bowls and cups eschew dowdy, same-same motifs for sexy sailors and well-endowed, semi-naked studs worthy of a Jean Genet novel. Original and provocative, they're a big hit with collectors from Berlin to San Francisco. Those who prefer their tea more tepid can opt for other themes, from energetic palms and marine creatures to colour-popping abstract patterns. All are made in Alessandro's tiny backroom studio using various techniques. Among these is sgraffito, an ancient process in which successive layers of contrasting glaze are applied before the surface is scratched to reveal the bottom glaze. Despite their kudos, items are affordable, with small bowls retailing for around €10. Oh, and if you're wondering about the original drawings and prints on the walls, they're Alessandro's creations too.

7 KALIMALA

Salizada San Lio 5387
041 528 3596
[MAP p. 166 C4]

In his cluttered, brightly lit atelier, Trieste-born Roberto Zuttion turns vegetable-tanned Tuscan leather into one-of-a-kind footwear and accessories for women and men. You might fall for a pair of 1930s-inspired lace-up flats, some funky sneaker-sole sandals or a hybrid sandal-shoe for the fashion forward. Subtle, unconventional details pimp many of his pieces: belts with hand-painted patterns or asymmetrical buckles, or 'lizard-skin' boots with thick, whip-stitch soles fit for modern Vikings. Accessories also include modish handbags, totes, duffel and carry-all bags, and you'll also find wallets and a handful of leather jackets. Prices are very reasonable given the quality and craftsmanship, with both men's and women's sandals from around €90 to €110, winter shoes around €140 to €190, and hand-painted belts for €70 or under. Note that the store is usually closed on Sundays in the colder months.

8 CERAMICHE CHIMERA

Salizzada dei Greci 3459
041 476 1809
[MAP p.164 C2]

Originally painting sets for plays and amusement parks, Ilaria Agesicora Rigoni's interest in ceramics was piqued by a ceramicist friend. After honing her skills in Nove – a Veneto town famous for its ceramics – Ilaria opened her own Venetian workshop, which stocks her quirky, contemporary wares. These include affordable, off-white ceramic cups, jugs, bowls and vases, playfully dented and streaked with bright pastel hues. The affable artist also produces dreamy watercolours and etchings of historical Venetian palaces, available both framed and unframed. Prices are equally democratic, with postcard-sized prints for those on restrictive budgets (or luggage allowances). The prints also make it onto leather-backed sleeves for eye glasses. If handcrafted jewellery is more your thing, seek out the colourful, enamel-and-copper earrings, made by Ilaria's friend Maite across the sea in Barcelona.

9 LIBRERIA ACQUA ALTA

Calle Lunga Santa Maria
Formosa 5176b
041 296 0841
[MAP p. 167 E3]

Only in Venice is the concept
of storing books in bathtubs,
fishing boats and gondolas
practical rather than odd.
Just ask bookstore 'High
Water', whose unconventional
storage system has come
in handy during floods. Its
tightly packed rooms are a
hoarding bookworm's Valhalla,
overflowing with old, new,
literary and popular titles,
from medieval history to pulp
fiction. Whatever room is left
is jammed with ephemera:
vintage and replica maps
and posters, art prints and
postcards, even old Italian
records. Miraculously, there's
still enough room for a cast
of friendly felines, including
a chilled-out tabby called
Tigre (Tiger). While there are
better curated bookstores in
Venice, I do love this place for
its flea-market vibe, random
finds (I once bought a fab
Cinzano poster here) and its
Instagrammable book steps out
the back. Cash only.

10 NEVODI

Via Garibaldi 1788–89
041 241 1136
[MAP p. 182 A2]

Any food blogger worth their salt will direct you to convivial, timber-beamed Nevodi (Venetian for 'Nephews'). One of Venice's most underrated bistros, the place just nails it, serving up honest, unfussed fare with high-end execution. While many locals drop in for cicheti (Venetian tapas), vino and a chat with owner Silvio Colauzzi at the bar, Nevodi merits your full attention, so phone to make a reservation and head in ravenous. From super-fresh crudo (raw fish) to baccalà (salted cod) prepared three ways, dishes are simple, classic and all about letting top-tier produce sing. Surf takes preference, with a handful of meat and vegetarian options that include artisan salumi (cured meats), a very Venetian dish of pan-fried calf livers with sautéed onions and seasonal, cult-status ravioli stuffed with earthy truffles. If it's on the menu, always conclude with nonna's old-school chocolate salami, best washed down with a fiery Veneto grappa.

POCKET TIP
If you're hankering for quality pizza, make a beeline for Nevodi spin-off Nevodi PizzaLab (Via Garibaldi 1341).

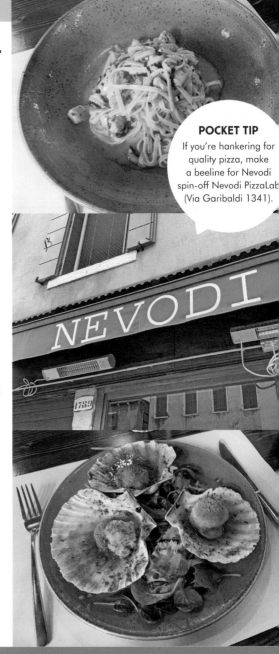

11 GIBRAN

Calle del Cafetier 6645
375 599 7676
[MAP p. 167 F2]

When I've had one too many
plates of bigoli, homely,
upbeat Gibran is my go-to
(and that of many Venetian
friends). Pointed Arabesque
wall niches glimpse out at a
painted aquamarine sea, an apt
backdrop for Middle Eastern
nosh that's fresh, authentic and
utterly delicious. In his open
kitchen, Lebanese chef Ibrahim
makes almost everything
from scratch, using quality
produce and his rank-and-file
of spice jars. Dunk flatbread
into creamy hummus and baba
ghanoush, tuck into golden
falafel and generous plates
of couscous, or opt for one of
my comfort staples: sheikh el
mehchi (zucchini stuffed with
minced beef, tomato, pine
nuts, mint and spices). While
the lamb dishes are especially
popular, herbivores will find
a good selection of meat-free
dishes, including succulent
warak inab (vine leaves stuffed
with rice, tomato, onion,
parsley and spices) and zesty
fattoush salad. Alcohol isn't
sold onsite, though you are
more than welcome to bring
your own.

POCKET TIP

Sporting a Palladio-designed
façade, the Renaissance Chiesa
di San Francesco della Vigna
(Campo San Francesco) houses
Fra Antonio da Negroponte's
only verified surviving work,
the glorious, mid-15th-
century *Madonna and
Child Enthroned*.

12 SALVMERIA

Via Giuseppe Garibaldi 1769
041 523 3971
[MAP p. 182 A2]

This former deli (note the original 'Salvmeria' sign above the entrance) is as good for a tipple as it is for a meal, with top-notch bites, interesting wines and thick, strong espresso more akin to Naples than Venice. Considered, produce-driven edibles range from bite-size cicheti (Venetian tapas) to heartier classics like pancetta coppata in saor (salt-cured pork belly in a sweet-and-sour sauce) and melanzana alla parmigiana con prosciutto (eggplant parmigiana with prosciutto). The latter, along with the arancini (fried rice balls) and the odd glass of Nero d'Avola, are a nod to co-owner Giorgio's Sicilian roots. Vino is well priced, regional and smaller-batch, and the cute, kiosk-like outdoor bar counter a good spot to strike up conversations with the locals. If you're peckish, order a platter of mixed cicheti or a board of artisan charcuterie and cheeses, the latter sourced from across Italy. And while reservations aren't generally required, it pays to call ahead if heading in Friday or Saturday night.

POCKET TIP

Hole-in-the-wall El Réfolo (Via Garibaldi 1580) is a local favourite for a quick bite or aperitivo, with craft brews, vino and quality bites like mini panini and cheese-and-charcuterie boards.

13 IN PARADISO

Giardini della Biennale 1260
041 241 3972
[MAP p. 182 B3]

In Paradiso provides a trio of precious commodities in this city: leafiness, space and open sky. Caught between the Giardini della Biennale and the sea, its mellow-yellow villa, shaded patio and lush, waterfront terrace channel a Riviera vibe. It's an especially wonderful spot for a drink during the Biennale, when culture vultures flock here to debrief, chill and, most importantly, to see and be seen. From 4pm, many opt for the daily spritz special, offered at an easy-drinking €10 per half litre. It's a perfect way to while away a few hours while reading a book, eavesdropping or (depending on your table) simply gazing out at Venice and the passing parade of vaporetti (ferries), fashionable locals and smitten tourists. And while you may be tempted to stay for a bite, there are better options for dinner, so sip away while making dinner plans for somewhere else.

POCKET TIP
For a novel break between Via Garibaldi and the Giardini della Biennale (Biennale Gardens), retreat to Serra dei Giardini (Viale Giuseppe Garibaldi 1254), a late-19th-century greenhouse turned cafe and nursery.

14 AL COVO

Campiello della Pescaria 3968
041 522 3812
[MAP p. 165 D3]

With fans including the late Anthony Bourdain, Al Covo is a food-lover's ideal: family run (by chef Cesare Benelli and his Texan wife Diane), with knowledgeable staff, warm, art-slung interiors and a menu that lists its Slow Food producers. Whether it's an amuse-bouche of buffalo-milk ricotta and wafer-thin pears, a primo of intensely flavoured linguine with local clams and zucchini, or a secondo of flawlessly grilled calamari on celeriac purée, the emphasis is always on superlative ingredients, prepared simply and exceptionally. High quality doesn't come cheap, though the good-value lunchtime 'Carte Blanche' set menu offers an appetiser, pasta dish, main course and dessert for €49. Set-menu choices are technically left to the chef, though it's always worth politely asking what's on offer as alternatives might be offered. Leave room for the exceptional desserts: the semifreddo of grappa, cinnamon, Corinth raisins and meringue-style pine nuts is unforgettable. Book at least four days in advance (ristorantealcovo.com) and note that it's only open Thursday to Monday.

POCKET TIP
Waterfront promenade Riva degli Schiavoni is especially beautiful for strolling early in the morning or at sunset.

ISOLA DI SAN GIORGIO MAGGIORE & GIUDECCA

Good things come in small packages, including the Isola di San Giorgio Maggiore. Not remotely intimidated by the architectural magnificence staring at it from San Marco across the basin, the island ups the ante with its own Chiesa di San Giorgio Maggiore (*see* p. 106), a stately Renaissance masterpiece designed by Andrea Palladio. Prodding its more famous rival, it too offers a red-brick, copper-crowned campanile (bell tower), just with better views. Converted into a military garrison by Napoleon in the 19th century and a cultural centre in the 20th century, the Monastero di San Giorgio Maggiore – home to the Fondazione Giorgio Cini (*see* p. 104) – claims lesser-known treasures. Among these is an elegant Palladian cloister and two extraordinary libraries.

Directly to the west, the long, thin island of Giudecca serves up unique Venetian streetscapes of brooding old factories, sleepy docks and criminally charming campielli (small squares) slung with hung laundry, potted plants and the odd football-chasing toseto (child). While it claims the glorious Palladian Chiesa del Santissimo Redentore (*see* p. 107), not to mention some notable contemporary galleries, Giudecca's real appeal lies in its atmospheric backstreets, lazy waterfront lunches and unobstructed city views.

Vaporetto (ferry) lines 2, 4.1 and 4.2 stop at all four Giudecca stops: Sacca Fisola, Palanca, Redentore and Zitelle. You can catch line 2 from San Marco–San Zaccaria to Isola di San Giorgio Maggiore and then continue on to Giudecca.

→ *Modern art and the Monastero di San Giorgio Maggiore*

1 FONDAZIONE GIORGIO CINI

Isola di San Giorgio Maggiore
041 271 0237
[MAP p. 175 F1]

Severely damaged by Napoleon during his occupation of Venice, the fascinating Benedictine Monastero di San Giorgio Maggiore found its saviour in cultured industrialist Vittorio Cini, who acquired it in 1951 and restored it in memory of his son Giorgio. One-hour tours of the complex take in two Renaissance cloisters, one designed by Palladio. The Renaissance architect also designed the monastery's vaulted cenacle, home to a facsimile of Veronese's monumental *The Wedding Feast in Cana*; the original now hangs in the Louvre. Baldassare Longhena takes credit for the grand staircase and **Longhena Library**, the latter one of two libraries visited. The other, the **Nuova Manica Lunga**, is a contemporary conversion of the monastery's former sleeping quarters. Guided tours (Thurs–Tues) also offer a peek at a clever garden maze dedicated to Argentinian writer Jorge Luis Borges. Book tickets online (cini.it) or at the ticket office, located left of the Chiesa di San Giorgio Maggiore.

POCKET TIP
Once known as the Isola dei Cipressi (Island of Cypresses) for its abundance of conifers, the island was donated by Doge Tribuno Memmo to the Benedictines in the late 10th century, who built the island's monastery.

2 CHIE/A DI /AN GIORGIO MAGGIORE

Isola di San Giorgio Maggiore
041 522 7827
[MAP p. 175 F1]

Many come here for the extraordinary views from the bell tower, but Andrea Palladio's genius is written all over the face of his 16th-century masterpiece. Look closely and you'll notice that the church's marble façade is composed of two overlaid façades: one tall and narrow, the other low and wide. The result is an innovative interplay of depth and geometrics considered a highlight of Palladio's illustrious career. Built between 1566 and 1610, the building replaces a much older Benedictine church, destroyed in an earthquake in 1223. Inside, Palladio's crisp grey-and-white interior is counterpointed by richly hued paintings that include Tintoretto's *The Last Supper* and *The Jews in the Desert*. Usually between May and November, the visual drama heats up further with the addition of contemporary art installations inside the complex. Whatever time of the year you visit, take the lift to the top of the basilica's late-18th-century campanile (bell tower) for a sweeping, soul-stirring panorama.

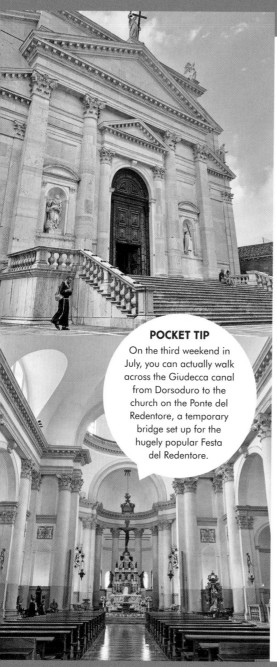

3 CHIE/A DEL /ANTI//IMO REDENTORE

Campo del SS Redentore 194,
Giudecca
[MAP p. 174 A4]

What better way to celebrate deliverance from the Black Death than with a starchitect-designed landmark called Church of the Most Holy Redeemer? That's exactly what the Venetian Senate thought, no doubt grateful for the quashing of a plague that claimed some 46,000 Venetians. Wisely, they entrusted Andrea Palladio with their vision, resulting in this Renaissance marvel. Although Palladio died in 1580, his foreman Antonio da Ponte (the designer of the Rialto Bridge) stayed true to the original designs, completing the church in 1592. The era is captured in Paolo Piazza's early 17th-century painting *Venice's Offering for Liberation for the Plague of 1575–77*, located above the entrance. It's one of several noteworthy artworks, among them Tintoretto's *The Flagellation of Christ*, located on the third altar to the right, and Veronese's altarpiece *The Baptism of Christ*.

POCKET TIP

On the third weekend in July, you can actually walk across the Giudecca canal from Dorsoduro to the church on the Ponte del Redentore, a temporary bridge set up for the hugely popular Festa del Redentore.

4 ARTI/TI ARTIGIANI DEL CHIO/TRO

Campo San Cosma 620a,
Giudecca
[MAP p. 172 B4]

Hidden away in Giudecca's
backstreets is this hub of
artisan workshops, located
in the 15th-century cloister
of Convento dei Santi Cosma
e Damiano. Workshops
open to the public include
that of Murano-born
glassmaker Stefano Morasso
(stefanomorasso.it), famous for
his colour-blending technique
and miniature creations. The
workshop is great for affordable
glass jewellery, a collaborative
effort with Stefano's
metalworking partner,
Nicoletta. Just email ahead
(info@stefanomorasso.it) if
stopping by on a Sunday as the
workshop is sometimes closed.
On the same side of the cloister
is Cartavenezia (cartavenezia.
it; open by appointment
only). Here, Campanian-born
Fernando di Masone crafts
tactile bookmarks, notebooks,
sketchbooks, photo albums
and Venice-themed cards
using handmade cotton paper.
Consider buying a trio of the
latter and framing them back
home. If money isn't an issue,
seek out his conversation-piece
necklaces, which might be in
the form of tiny paper leaves
inscribed with poetry.

POCKET TIP
In a neo-Gothic palazzo,
Giudecca gallery Casa dei Tre Oci
(Fondamenta de le Zitelle 43) hosts
top-tier photography exhibitions,
including retrospectives of greats
like David LaChapelle and
Jacques Henri Lartigue.

5 LA PALANCA

Fondamenta Sant'Eufemia 448,
Giudecca
041 528 7719
[MAP p. 172 C4]

Punters love no-frills La
Palanca for numerous reasons:
its waterfront address,
affable staff, solid cooking at
reasonable (for the location)
prices. While I don't feel that
the food here always quite hits
the mark, there is something
irrefutably feel good about
long alfresco lunches by the
Giudecca canal, Venice spread
out before you like a Canaletto
canvas. Call a day ahead to
secure a waterside table, the
best spot to tuck into dishes
like sea-bass ravioli and
cuttlefish-ink polenta. Outside
the peak summer season, you
can always simply head in a
few minutes before noon and
try your luck for a table too.
Either way, watch out for the
small random splashes when
the vaporetti (ferries) chug
past; keep your feet on the
wooden crates provided. Lunch
is served between noon and
2.30pm. For the rest of the
time, the place is a laid-back
neighbourhood bar, nourishing
the islanders with coffee,
spritzes and decent cicheti
(Venetian tapas).

6 SKYLINE

Hilton Molino Stucky Venice
Giudecca 810
041 272 3316
[MAP p. 172 A3]

If you get caught between
the moon and Venice city,
chances are you're downing
drinks at this eighth-floor bar,
the loftiest in town. Crowning
a brick Gothic-Revival flour-
mill-turned-Hilton, its terrace
panorama is simply inimitable.
Cupolas and bell towers
punctuate a skyline view
that includes Venice's most
famous basilica bell towers, the
Baroque dome of the Basilica
Santa Maria della Salute (*see*
p. 70), and even some of the
lagoon's southern islands.
While drinks aren't cheap
(expect to pay around €15 for a
spritz or €10 to €15 for a glass
of vino), they're well mixed
and well worth the bewitching
backdrop, especially as day
melts into night. If the bar isn't
taking reservations, head up an
hour before sunset for a better
chance of claiming one of the
coveted bar tables close to the
terrace edge. It's the best spot
to watch as La Serenissima
slips into her glittering
evening cloak.

MURANO & ISOLA DI SAN MICHELE

Since the late 13th century, Murano has been synonymous with glass-blowing, its artisans firing, rolling and shaping some of the world's most revered glassware. The compact, connected islands that make up Murano claim a plethora of glass workshops and showrooms, stocking everything from traditional Venetian chandeliers to contemporary tableware and mid-century design collectables. While these are spread across the islands, you'll find a concentration of vendors on Fondamenta dei Vetrai and Fondamenta Manin (split by the canal, Rio dei Vetrai), as well as on Riva Longa. At its eastern end, Riva Longa snaps into Fondamenta Marco Giustinian, which shoots north-east towards Murano's two cultural drawcards: the Museo del Vetro (Museum of Glass, *see* p. 115) and the Basilica dei SS Maria e Donato (*see* p. 114). While the former explores the evolution of the island's most famous craft, the latter – one of the oldest churches in the lagoon – harbours astounding 12th-century mosaics.

Less frequented by tourists is brooding Isola di San Michele. Wedged between Murano and the city, this is Venice's main cemetery, Cimitero di San Michele (*see* p. 116), providing eternal rest since 1807. If it's solitude you're seeking, this tranquil island delivers.

From Fondamente Nove in Cannaregio, vaporetto (ferry) 4.1 stops at both Isola di San Michele (Cimitero) and Murano. Line 3 runs directly between Murano, Piazzale Roma (bus station) and Ferrovia outside Venezia Santa Lucia (train station).

→1 *Murano glassblower demonstrating his skills*

SIGHTS
1. Basilica dei SS Maria e Donato
2. Museo del Vetro (Museum of Glass)
3. Cimitero di San Michele

SHOPPING
4. ElleElle
5. Cesare Toffolo

EATING & DRINKING
6. Osteria al Duomo
7. Trattoria Busa alla Torre

113

1 BASILICA DEI SS MARIA E DONATO

Campo San Donato
[MAP p. 181 E1]

Legend has it that the bones dangling inside Murano's basilica are those of a dragon, slain by brave St Darius of Arezzo. The remains of both victim and victor were interred here in 1125, looted from Kefalonia by Venetian Doge Domenico Michiel. While the jury is still out on the dragon bones, there's no doubting the extraordinary beauty of the basilica itself, whose origins lie in the 7th century. Before entering, note the apse's unusual hexagonal shape and its decorative arched loggias (balconies) and colourful marble bands, the latter two reminiscent of a Byzantine doll's house. Inside, Murano glassmaking dazzles in the apse's 12th-century mosaic of the Virgin Mary. It's a worthy match for the storybook floor mosaics, a Byzantine menagerie of animals vividly depicting everything from grazing peacocks to a couple of chickens carrying a hapless fox.

2 MUSEO DEL VETRO (MUSEUM OF GLASS)

Fondamenta Giustinian 8
041 243 4914
[MAP p. 181 E1]

To delve into Murano's artisan glass history, slip into Museo del Vetro. A design and history museum in one, it explores both the origins and evolution of glass making and houses a collection of spectacular decorative arts. Exhibits touch on numerous eras, techniques and products, among them Venetian beads, for centuries a powerful trading currency between Europe and Africa. The museum's inventory includes millennia-old vases and jewellery, as well as a rare 18th-century glass garden, modelled on traditional Italian garden design and complete with dainty glass hedges, flowers and fountains. If you're a design buff, the temporary exhibitions can be especially interesting, often showcasing modern designers and artists (one retrospective explored the legacy of 20th-century Finnish designer Tapio Wirkkala).
The museum itself occupies the Palazzo Giustinian, home to the bishops of Torcello between 1689 and 1805.
In the first-floor main hall, note the Rococo fresco by artist Francesco Zugno.

3 CIMITERO DI SAN MICHELE

Isola di San Michele
041 729 2841
[MAP p. 179 E1]

For the living, the sombre walls
of Venice's main cemetery
promise an atmospheric oasis
of sleepy, verdant pathways
and famous tombstones. Before
exploring the island and its
eclectic mausoleums and
temples, pick up a free map
from the information office by
the entrance. It marks, albeit
not always precisely, the graves
of well-known figures, among
them Russian composer Igor
Stravinsky and Ballets Russes
founder Sergei Diaghilev, both
of whom rest in the Greek
section. Fans of American
literature will find Ezra Pound
in the Evangelist section,
flanked by the poet's mistress,
concert violinist Olga Rudge.
For contemporary architecture,
seek out the Modernist
courtyards designed by British
architect David Chipperfield.
While the cemetery dates
from the early 19th century,
the island's history is much
older: its 15th-century **Chiesa
di San Michele in Isola**
is one of Venice's earliest
Renaissance churches, while
the adjoining cloister belonged
to a Camaldolese monastery
whose residents included
medieval cartographer
Fra Mauro.

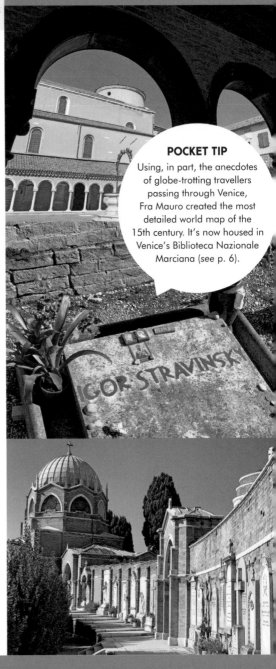

POCKET TIP

Using, in part, the anecdotes
of globe-trotting travellers
passing through Venice,
Fra Mauro created the most
detailed world map of the
15th century. It's now housed in
Venice's Biblioteca Nazionale
Marciana (see p. 6).

4 ELLEELLE

Fondamenta Manin 52
041 527 4866
[MAP p. 180 C3]

The late Umberto Nason is considered a maverick of avant-garde glass making on Murano. Represented in A-list galleries such as New York's MoMA (Museum of Modern Art), the artist's 1955 Lidia line won the Compasso d'Oro, Italy's coveted industrial-design award. With white exteriors and contrasting colour interiors, the range of Lidia bowls, plates and cups are available instore, with small bowls retailing for €70 a pop. Nason's classic pieces sit side by side with more recent glassware designs from the NasonMoretti workshop, including the Guepiere range of slinky, dual-colour flutes and wine glasses. All objects are signed and numbered, with stock also including decanters, jugs, vases, tealight holders and lamps. Those on strict budgets can pick up contemporary glass rings for around €20.

POCKET TIP
When shopping for glassware, support Murano artisans by buying items labelled 'Vetro Artistico Murano'.

5 CESARE TOFFOLO

Fondamenta Vetrai 37
041 73 64 60
[MAP p. 180 B4]

Among master glass-blowers, Cesare Toffolo is a virtual superstar, his inimitable creations appearing in galleries from Tokyo to Pittsburgh. Few people have mastered the lume (lampwork) technique like this guy, one in which blowtorch-melted rods of glass are shaped into breathtakingly delicate creations. In Cesare's case, these include peacocks with spun-glass tails perched on decorative vases and replicas of old-school Murano chandeliers. The attention to detail is gobsmacking, with miniature chandeliers taking up to a month to complete. Beyond these are more practical glass creations, from hip modern tumblers, shot glasses and bowls, to eye-catching jewellery. These include simple, petite earrings made of glass, crystal and silver leaf for under €15. Note that Toffolo is usually closed from mid-January to mid-February.

PLEASE
NOT TOUCH

FINE
CE

POCKET TIP
If it's open, head upstairs to peek at the small in-house gallery, showcasing some of Cesare's conversation pieces.

6 OSTERIA AL DUOMO

Fondamenta Maschio 20-21
041 527 4303
[MAP p. 181 E1]

I must confess: Venetian pizza doesn't make me go gaga. My (biased) idea of pizza perfection is wood-fired, bubbling and Neapolitan. That said, I actually *do* like the pie served at this Murano tavern. In fact, I'd say it's one of the best in the lagoon, with a base that's crisp, thin and satisfyingly textured. The offerings are mind boggling, with almost 100 pizzas to 'umm' and 'ahh' over, including a generous number of vegetarian options. I usually play favourites with the spicy, salami-topped Cooperativa, named for the osteria's curious backstory. The place was opened as a co-op grocery store by the parish priest in 1903. More than a century later, it's still owned by 50 local families, its terrazzo floors, chintzy lighting and vest-clad waiters a comforting, old-school sight. Pie aside, the menu includes homemade tagliolini and tagliatelle pasta, best savoured in the leafy back garden. Phone to book ahead on weekends, especially in the winter, when space is more limited.

7 TRATTORIA BUSA ALLA TORRE

Campo Santo Stefano 3,
Murano
041 73 96 62
[MAP p. 180 C2]

Lording over this timber-beamed, lunch-only stalwart is larger-than-life owner-chef Gabriele Masiol. Locals fondly know him as 'Lele il Rosso' (Lele The Red), a reference to his ruddy complexion. Don't be surprised if he comes up to your table for a bit of banter, recounting stories of travel adventures and life. Lele's food is unapologetically rustic and surf-centric: think bigoli in salsa (thick spaghetti with anchovy and onion sauce), scampi e calamari fritti (fried prawns and calamari) and slow-cooked seppie alla veneziana (squid-ink cuttlefish with polenta). In the cooler months, comfort comes in the form of a moreish zuppa di pesce (fish soup), while the handful of meaty options include my own nonna Nori's favourite, fegato alla veneziana (Venetian-style calf livers with simmered onions). Despite being called a 'tourist menu', the two-course €15.50 special doesn't skimp on quality. In the warmer months, head in early for a table on the campo (square).

POCKET TIP

For an afternoon drink with the islanders, drop by Sottovento (Riva Longa 27), an osteria that also serves good-value cheese-and-charcuterie boards. Note the floor, made of upcycled bricole (lagoon navigation poles).

BURANO, MAZZORBO & TORCELLO

Set in the Northern Lagoon, this trio of islands reward those who spend longer in the city, serving up a saltier, more bucolic slice of Venetian life. Burano pulls the biggest crowds, its low-rise, colour-popping buildings big on idiosyncratic charm. Traditional, handmade lace is its other claim to fame, with vendors lining its bustling commercial spine, Via Galuppi. That said, much of the stock sold these days is machine made and imported, so look for lace labelled 'Fatto a Burano' (Made in Burano). Stray off the strip and you'll encounter a more genuine side to this working-class fishing island, one of languorous squares, dusty vegetable gardens and reserved, sharp-eyed old timers. Burano is also famous for its bussolai buranelli (ring-shaped butter cookies), best sampled at cult-status bakery-patisserie Panificio Pasticceria Carmelina Palmisano (see p. 130).

From the north-west tip of Burano, a pedestrian bridge leads to tranquil Mazzorbo, fawned over by gourmands for its Michelin-starred restaurant, Venissa Ristorante & Osteria (see p. 132) and its one-of-a-kind vineyard. The latter is planted with Dorona di Venezia, a local grape rediscovered in a forlorn garden in 2002. That garden lies on marshy Torcello, a five-minute ferry ride from Burano. Torcello was the first island settled in the lagoon, by 5th-century Veneto mainlanders fleeing Attila the Hun's marauding antics. Sleepy and rural, it was once a busy medieval trading centre. Attesting to these long-gone halcyon days is the Basilica di Santa Maria Assunta (see p. 124), the oldest Byzantine–Romanesque structure in the lagoon and home to dramatic, tale-telling mosaics.

Vaporetti (ferries) bound for Burano, Mazzorbo and Torcello leave from Fondamente Nove in Cannaregio, taking around 35 to 45 minutes to reach the islands.

→ *A typically colourful building on Burano*

SIGHTS
1. Basilica di Santa Maria Assunta

SIGHTS & SHOPPING
2. Dalla Lidia

SHOPPING
3. Alessandro Tagliapietra Fine Art Photography
4. Emilia Burano

EATING & DRINKING
5. Osteria Al Museo
6. Panificio Pasticceria Carmelina Palmisano
7. Venissa Ristorante & Osteria
8. Taverna Tipica Veneziana

123

1 BASILICA DI SANTA MARIA ASSUNTA

Piazza Torcello, Torcello
041 73 01 19
[MAP p. 183 C1]

Built in the 7th century, expanded in the 9th century, then rebuilt in the early 11th century, Torcello's basilica still knocks visitors for six. Not only is it the oldest Venetian Byzantine church in the lagoon, its golden mosaics are the earliest in Venice. The serene 11th-century apse mosaic – starring the Madonna, her holy offspring and 12 apostles standing in a field of local poppies – provides sharp contrast to the nail-biting action unfurling above the basilica's main entrance. Here, soaring 11th and 12th-century mosaics capture Christ's crucifixion, resurrection and scenes from the Last Judgement; among them a child Antichrist sitting in Hades's lap. Unless you're especially keen on exploring local archaeological finds at the small **Museo Provinciale** next door, opt for the basilica and bell-tower combo (€9), the latter providing a uniquely rustic lagoon panorama. To the right of the basilica stands the round, 11th-century **Chiesa di Santa Fosca**.

2 DALLA LIDIA

Via Galuppi 215, Burano
041 73 00 52
[MAP p. 183 C4]

Exuding the charm of an
old haberdasher, family-run
Dalla Lidia has been vending
lace since the 1940s. What I
especially love about the place
is its historical collection of
lacework, tucked away at the
back of the store. Illustrating
the craft's evolution over the
centuries, its cachet includes
pieces from the 17th century
and an outrageously elaborate
frock from the 19th century,
reputedly made for a princess.
If you're not too fussed about
delving deep into lacemaking's
backstory, a trip here instead
of the island's ticketed Museo
del Merletto will suffice.
Dalla Lidia's own stock is all
handmade, either on Burano
or in other parts of Italy and
Europe. Prices aren't cheap but
the quality is high: placemats
retail from €50, with tablecloths
and super-cute kids' outfits
from around €200. At the
front of the store, keep an eye
out for the framed lacework
depiction of *The Last Supper*;
the fruit of one whole year of
patient threading.

3 ALESSANDRO TAGLIAPIETRA FINE ART PHOTOGRAPHY

Via San Martino sx 236, Burano
347 167 5203
[MAP p. 183 B4

Although Alessandro Tagliapietra still blows glass in his native Murano, the Burano-based creative is at his happiest behind the lens. An award-winning photographer, he's especially passionate about what he calls 'slow photography'; quiet, meditative, long-exposure shots. The end results are powerful, often brooding portraits of Venice: palaces reflected in inky acqua alta (tide peak), silent canals shrouded in fog, and the moody shades of the lagoon itself. Not surprisingly, Alessandro's favourite seasons are autumn and winter, when it's not unusual to find him out on the water, pelted by rain or snow, capturing photographs already imprinted in his mind. Prices are reasonable, with some of the smallest framed prints costing around €20 and postcards a bargain €1.

POCKET TIP
To see some of Alessandro's glasswork (and that of his brother Denis), check out his glass shop Tagliapietra around the corner (Rio Terra di Pizzo 222).

4 EMILIA BURANO

Piazza Galuppi 205, Burano
041 73 52 45
[MAP p. 183 C4]

Not every store comes with a 'Wall of Stars'. But then, not every store counts Uma Thurman, Julia Roberts and Kate Hudson among its clientele. Despite the fame, Emilia remains a family-run enterprise, producing some of the most sought-after lacework and fine linens in Italy. At the helm is fourth-generation designer Lorenzo Ammendola, whose collections include collaborations with Aston Martin, Baccarat and Fendi. The bedsheet sets are the epitome of understated chic, though prices do start at a VIP €500. More accessible items include stylish linen table runners and placemats, which retail for around €25 a piece. Even if you're not in the market for high-end textiles, it's worth dropping by to view the small upstairs museum, where intriguing items include 15th-century lace dresses and rather genial lace renditions of Venetian palaces, designed by Lorenzo himself.

POCKET TIP
Laguna Fla (lagunaflaline.it) sails between Burano and the Isola di San Francesco del Deserto, where friars lead Italian-language tours of their verdant monastic home (sanfrancescodeldeserto.it). Call 347 9922959 to book a boat ride.

5 OSTERIA AL MUSEO

Piazza Baldassarre Galuppi
113-115, Burano
041 73 50 12
[MAP p. 183 C4]

There's a lot of love behind this sunny, piazza-side restaurant, a 'sea change' of sorts for mates Tommaso Chinellato and Carlo Salini. While the vibe is casual and convivial, the obsession with quality is strict, from the fine-pedigree waiters (some hailing from top Venetian hotels and restaurants) to the summer-only white-peach Bellini, made to order. Market-fresh fish, local meats, house-made pasta and vegetables grown in Veneto soil shape the menu, a surf-focussed fusion of regional traditions and contemporary finesse. The antipasto di pesce (seafood antipasto platter) is filling enough for lunch, with other worthy choices including house-made gnocchetti (small gnocchi) served with prized red prawns (both raw and cooked), as well as Burano's classic risotto di gò, made with the lagoon's famed goby fish. Phone a day ahead and always check opening times as they tend to fluctuate.

POCKET TIP

Opposite the osteria, the 16th-century Chiesa di San Martino houses Giambattista Tiepolo's 1725 painting *The Crucifixion* and an arresting 19th-century Russian icon known as *Madonna di Kazan*.

129

6 PANIFICIO PASTICCERIA CARMELINA PALMISANO

Via Galuppi 335, Burano
041 73 00 10
[MAP p. 183 B4]

Burano is famous for bussolai buranelli (ring-shaped butter cookies) and this bakery–patisserie is the best place to get your greedy mitts on them. In business since 1928, it's reassuringly old-school, lorded over by glam matriarch Carmelina Palmisano and drawing steady streams of signore (ladies) restocking their pantries. While the cookies themselves are simple (flour, butter, sugar, egg yolks, vanilla and salt), they're ridiculously addictive, so don't be surprised if you plough through a pack in one sitting. Other Venetian treats sold here include choc chip–studded bricole (named after the wooden navigation poles punctuating the lagoon) and raisin-studded zaletti (cornmeal cookies). If you're a choc-nut tragic, try the peverini, chocolate cookies pimped with chopped peanuts. Gluten-free baked goods are also available.

7 VENISSA RISTORANTE & OSTERIA

Fondamenta Santa Caterina 3, Mazzorbo
041 527 2281
[MAP p. 183 A3]

It's easy to imagine other restaurants seething at Venissa. There's the Michelin star *and* the location; a walled vineyard with a 14th-century bell tower, and prized vines of native Dorano di Venezia. Produce from the garden and surrounding waters dictate edgy menus, concocted by forward-thinking chefs, Francesco Brutto and Chiara Pavan. The result: palate-wowing pairings like raw seam bream with apricot, thyme, cashew and razor clam, or ravioli with wormwood butter, bitter herbs and pine nuts. If you can't splash serious euros at the restaurant – best booked three to four weeks ahead – secure a table at Venissa's more casual, bistro-style osteria. The dishes are simpler but made with the same premium produce. Try the popular twist on sarde in saor (sweet-and-sour sardines), which gives the fish some unexpected crunch. Walk-ins at the osteria are generally welcome, though it's smart to book a day or two ahead (venissa.it), especially for dinner and on weekends.

POCKET TIP
If you're a wine lover, call a week ahead to book a wine degustation (€25), which includes a tour of the vineyard with Venissa's sommelier.

8 TAVERNA TIPICA VENEZIANA

Fondamenta dei Borgognoni 5,
Torcello
370 357 0838
[MAP p. 183 B1]

In the warmer months, I love kicking back on a deckchair at this alfresco trattoria, shades on and Moretti in hand. It's especially popular on summer weekends (so head in early) and feels like a big communal backyard, with shaded tables and play equipment for kids. There's nothing fancy about the place. Food is lined up cafeteria-style, with the day's bites handwritten on butchers' paper. Options are rustic, tasty and seafood focussed; anything from oven-baked branzino (sea bass) and fritto misto (deep-fried mixed seafood) to grilled vegetables. There's also a dedicated (albeit modest) menu for vegetarians and vegans, offering simple grub like spaghetti con pomodoro (spaghetti with tomato) and a vegan burger. Of course, the place is just as good for a simple, lazy drink in the sun.

133

PADUA

Despite its proximity to Venice, Padua (Padova in Italian) refuses to lie in La Serenissima's shadow. Wealthy, confident and erudite, the city has played a powerful role in Italian history. It was here that renegade scholars founded the country's second-oldest university in 1222, a university whose scholars and students have included Galileo, Copernicus and playwright Carlo Goldoni. It was also here that Tuscan painter Giotto di Bondone planted the seeds of the Renaissance with his revolutionary frescoes in Cappella degli Scrovegni (*see* p. 136). Legend has it that Padua was founded by Trojan prince Antenor. First mentioned in 302 BCE, the city would become an influential Italian commune between the 11th and 13th centuries, drawing many illustrious figures. Among them literary greats Dante, Petrarch and Boccaccio, as well as Portuguese-born miracle-maker St Anthony of Padua, laid to rest under Byzantine Paduan domes.

Many centuries on, the Veneto's third-largest city remains an energetic university town. Grand piazzas and arcaded streets buzz with students, academics and bourgeois padovani (Paduans), sipping cappucini and spritzes, perusing produce on its central market squares, and exchanging thoughts on elegant Prato della Valle (*see* p. 136), one of Europe's largest public squares.

Trains are the easiest way to reach Padua, with regular departures from Venice Santa Lucia station and, on the mainland, Venezia Porto Marghera and Venezia-Mestre stations. Travel time is around 15 to 50 minutes. If driving, take the Torino-Trieste A4 freeway; check online (autostrade.it) to calculate tolls, payable by cash or carte (cards) at tollgates. Central Padua is a ZTL (Limited Traffic Zone), though non-resident motorists can drop off luggage at their hotel. If you're wanting to explore the city at a more leisurely place, consider an overnight stay (*see* p. 139).

→ *Detail from Rogier van der Weyden's Deposition, Musei Civici agli Eremitani*

POCKET TIP

The PadovaCard (from €16) offers one adult and one child under 14 access to most of Padua's attractions, plus use of city buses and trams. See online (turismopadova.it) for details.

SIGHTS

Padua's **Cappella degli Scrovegni** (Piazza Eremitani 8) claims one of the world's great seminal artworks: a cycle fresco by Giotto di Bondone. Executed between 1303 and 1305, its relatable, humanistic depiction of saints and sinners helped catapult Western art out of the Middle Ages and towards the Renaissance. The work was commissioned by banker Enrico Scrovegni, reputedly as atonement for usury. His own father was so infamous a money lender that he made it into Dante's *Divine Comedy*, as a figure in the Seventh Circle of Hell. While tickets to the chapel can be purchased at the neighbouring **Musei Civici agli Eremitani**, reserve tickets online (cappelladegliscrovegni.it) in advance as availability is limited.

The Musei Civici agli Eremitani houses local archaeological finds and artworks by Guariento, Bellini, Titian, Tintoretto and Veronese. Look for Giorgio Fossati's *Corsa dei fantini in Prato della Valle*, which captures Padua's famous elliptical piazza in the 18th century.

The **Prato della Valle** itself lies a 20-minute walk south of the museum. The 78 statues flanking the piazza's canal depict illustrious figures linked to the city. The 10 empty

pedestals once supported 10 Venetian doges, pulled down at Napoleon's behest after he seized control of Venice in 1797. A short walk east of the square lie two other Paduan highlights: the UNESCO World Heritage-listed **Orto Botanico** (Via dell'Orto Botanico 15) and the **Basilica di Sant'Antonio** (Piazza del Santo). While the former includes a 16th-century palm mentioned in Goethe's *Italian Journey*, the latter stores the remains of St Anthony of Padua. Florentine sculptor Donatello created the reliefs decorating the basilica's high altar.

Like the basilica, Padua's **Palazzo della Ragione** (Piazza delle Erbe) has its origins in the 13th century. Its medieval Salone (Great Hall) is awash with early-15th-century frescoes by Giusto de' Menabuoi and Nicolò Miretto. The frescoes were partially inspired by the astrological theories of Pietro d'Abano, a 13th-century professor at Padua University. The university's seat is the nearby Renaissance-era **Palazzo Bo** (Via VIII Febbraio 2). Here, 45-minute guided tours take in the Aula Magna (Great Hall) – where Galileo once lectured – as well as the world's first anatomy theatre. Tour times can be sporadic; check ahead online (unipd.it/en/bo).

PADUA

EATING & DRINKING

Padua's dining scene extends from cheap, cheerful student digs and street-food vendors, to atmospheric trattorias and restaurants serving regional specialties.

Stendhal, Lord Byron and Ernest Hemingway have all refueled at haughty **Caffè Pedrocchi** (Via VIII Febbraio 15), trading at this address since 1831. It's a grand affair, lavished with chandeliers and anecdotes. These include a bullet hole in the cafe's Sala Bianca (White Room), fired by Austro–Hungarian troops at students revolting against Habsburg rule in 1848. While you can dine here, it's best for its signature Caffè Pedrocchi alla menta (espresso with mint-flavoured cream and cocoa powder).

A better dining option is Padua's oldest tavern, **Da Nana della Giulia** (Via Santa Sofia 1). Local market produce dictates earthy regional dishes like orzotto (pearl-barley risotto) with mushrooms and pork sausage. There's usually one vegetarian offering per course and a well-curated wine list focused on Italy's north-east. Dinner reservations are essential (049 66 07 42). For something lighter, hit boho-spirited wine bar **Enoteca Il Tira Bouchon** (Sotto Il Salone 23/24), located under the arches of Palazzo della Ragione.

POCKET TIP

Under Palazzo della Ragione's arcade is La Folperia (Piazza della Frutta 1). A famous street-food vendor, it serves market-fresh seafood like folpo (octopus), best washed down with a bubbly prosecco.

⌡LEEPING

Hotels in the city generally lack X-factor, though comfortable, hospitable options are available. One standout is **Casa Giotto** (Via Porciglia 15), an impeccably modish B&B at budget-hotel prices. Both the rooms and communal areas are worthy of a *Monocle* magazine spread, decked out in beautiful artworks, mid-century design and striking bathrooms. Best of all, it's a short walk from Cappella degli Scrovegni (*see* p. 136).

If you have time, your own wheels and prefer something altogether more bucolic, opt for **Agriturismo Barchessa** (Via Cappuccini 9, Este), which offers highly affordable, self-catering apartments in a neoclassical villa, 37 kilometres (23 miles) south-west of central Padua. The property sits at the southern foot of the Colli Euganei (Euganean Hills), famed for their thermal spas and vineyards.

FIELD TRIP

VICENZA

It was Andrea Palladio who transformed Vicenza into an architectural show pony. Inspired by the equilibrious style of classical Roman architecture, the 16th-century architect bestowed the city and its rolling hills with palazzi, villas and churches long considered Renaissance highlights. Consequently, Vicenza and its Palladian villas are now UNESCO World Heritage–listed, drawing aesthetes from around the globe. And yet, the Veneto's fourth-largest city is more than its stately columns, porticoes and rotundas. It's also one of Italy's most elegant and livable cities, with a compact centro storico (historic centre) punctuated by art, bistros, boutiques and well-heeled vicentini (Vicenza locals) gliding by on bicycles. Cobbled streets lead to top-tier exhibitions, craft brews and Vicenza's most celebrated dish: milk-poached stockfish.

Vicenza's bullseye is lively Piazza dei Signori (see p. 142), a spacious square flanked by Palladio's copper-domed Basilica Palladiana and skyscraping Gothic bell tower Torre Bissara. Come Tuesday and Thursday mornings, market stalls flood the piazza, peddling everything from leather handbags to suede boots. Only 2 kilometres (1.2 miles) to the south, city streets give way to cypress-brushed hills, their quiet, winding roads leading to famously frescoed villas and dreamy valley views.

From Venice, Vicenza is a 45- to 80-minute train trip on the main line running between Venice and Milan. The line also services Padua and Verona. Opt for a Regionale Veloce service, which costs the same as the slower Regionale trains. See online (trenitalia.com) for details. The Torino-Trieste A4 freeway connects the city to Padua, Venice and Verona. Central Vicenza is a ZTL (Limited Traffic Zone); see online (comune.vicenza.it) for more information.

→ *Bucolic view from Villa Valmarana ai Nani*

SIGHTS

Unsurprisingly, many of Vicenza's must-sees are connected to architect Andrea Palladio. Get your bearings on **Piazza dei Signori**, dominated by the **Basilica Palladiana**. Once home to law courts and the city's Council of Four Hundred, the building is an architectural Kinder Surprise. Peer behind Palladio's 16th-century marble loggias and you'll discover the building's original Gothic façade, dating from the 15th century. Neighbouring **Torre Bissara** is even older, erected in 1174 and raised to its current height of 82 metres (269 feet) in the mid-15th century. The basilica's upstairs salone (Grand Hall) hosts excellent art exhibitions throughout the year, while its **Museo del Gioiello** (Jewellery Museum) explores both historic and contemporary jewellery design.

Within easy walking distance is **Teatro Olimpico** (Piazza Matteotti 11), Palladio's swan song. The architect's sudden death in 1580 saw the theatre completed by Vincenzo Scamozzi, who added the remarkable wooden stage set. Modelled on the ancient Greek city of Thebes, the set cleverly plays on perspective to give an impressive illusion of depth. The theatre is open to the public and continues to stage events, from theatre to opera and jazz.

POCKET TIP

The €15 Card 4 Musei pass offers entry to four city attractions from a list of 10. It's good value, especially given a single ticket to Teatro Olimpico is €11.

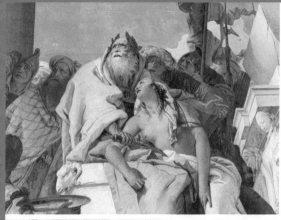

See teatrolimpicovicenza.it for details.

Nearby **Palazzo Leoni Montanari** (Contrà di Santa Corona 2 5) serves up artworks in the frescoed digs of a 17th-century textile merchant, including ancient pottery from Magna Graecia, paintings by 18th-century Venetian masters (including Canaletto) and the largest collection of Russian icons in Western Europe. It's also where you'll find Agostino Fasolato's jaw-dropping *The Fall of the Rebel Angels*, a cascade of combatting angels and demons carved from a single block of Carrara marble.

Some 1.6 kilometres (1 mile) south of central Vicenza, the gentle slopes of the Colli Berici (Berici Hills) are home to the aristocratic **Villa Valmarana ai Nani** (Via dei Nani 8), an elegant estate guarded by 17 curious stone nani (dwarves). While the historic gardens and views are gorgeous, the clincher is the large-scale frescoes by Giambattista Tiepolo and son Domenico. From the villa, a tranquil path leads downhill to one of Italy's most admired Renaissance palazzi, **La Rotonda** (Villa della Rotonda 45). Designed by Palladio, completed by Scamozzi, the villa's own frescoes were created by Alessandro and Giovanni Battista Maganza and Anselmo Canera.

EATING & DRINKING

Vicenza is famous for baccalà alla vicentina, (Vicentine-style stockfish) and you'll find a smashing version at **Gastronomia Il Ceppo** (Corso Andrea Palladio 196), a gourmet deli laden with salumi (cured meats), formaggi (cheeses), condiments, marinated vegetables and more. Its exceptional range of vini might include rare, spicy local Gruajo or a lesser-known Amarone brought in by the winemaker himself, muddy boots and all. Bottles line the deli's subterranean, lunch-only bistro, **Sòtobotega**, a favourite spot to savour polished dishes like bigoli pasta with duck ragù and orange zest.

Those seeking momentary respite from Veneto classics should make dinner reservations at **FuoriModena** (Contrà San Gaetano da Thiene 8; 0444 33 09 94), where a beautifully executed menu celebrates Italy's Emilia-Romagna region.

For coffee, aperitivo and regular evening jazz, swing by **Bar Borsa** (Piazza dei Signori 26). For saisons and session IPAs, hit svelte **Helmut** (Contrà Zanella 8), which also serves high-quality burgers (including vegan and vegetarian versions).

ſLEEPING

An overnight stay means more time to soak up Vicenza's understated magnetism. Mid-priced slumber spots include the centrally located **Palazzo Valmarana Braga** (Corso Antonio Fogazzaro 16), set in a Palladio-designed building speckled with frescoes, antiques and quality linen. Classic simplicity underscores its seven, multi-sized apartments, all of which come with a handy kitchen for cooking simple meals.

If you fancy snoozing in a 600-year-old abode once owned by a count, check-in at the very affordable B&B **Portico Rosso** (Contrà San Rocco 28), an 850 metre (2788 feet) walk from Piazza dei Signori. The vibe is homely, with crackling fires, comfortable sofas, art and curios from around the globe. All three guestrooms make for blissful retreats; the double 'Diana' comes with garden view and jacuzzi, while the single 'Maelis' includes a hand-carved bed once belonging to the count's wife.

VERONA

Fair Verona is so much more than quixotic Shakespearian lovebirds. Pressed up against a bend in Italy's second-longest river, the Adige, the city is spirited, cultured and intriguing in its own right. Roman gates and bridges, medieval towers and Renaissance palazzi litter its UNESCO World Heritage–listed historic centre. Together, they reveal the long backstory of a city at European crossroads ruled at different times by Ostrogoths, Lombards and Austrians. It's a city of photogenic squares, pretty side streets, leafy balconies and, in the case of Piazza delle Erbe (*see* p. 148), vivid, frescoed façades.

Directly across the river, fertile slopes rise up in a symphony of villas, ruins and historic gardens. This is Verona's quieter 'Left Bank', Veronetta (Little Verona). While the name sounds endearing today, its use in the early 19th century was belittling, coined by invading French troops to describe the side of the river occupied by the Austrians. Centuries on, the neighbourhood rewards the curious with commanding views of Verona's tightly-packed terracotta rooftops. It's a panorama fit for a town well-versed in the finer things, whether it be summer arias in the Roman Arena di Verona (*see* p. 148) or year-round feasting in prized eateries and wine bars.

Verona is a 70-minute express-train trip from Venice. Choose a Regionale Veloce train, which is quicker than a Regionale service. From the main train station (Verona Porta Nuova), Verona Airlink buses run to Verona Villafranca Airport (aeroportoverona.it), servicing flights to Italian and selected European destinations. If driving, the Torino-Trieste A4 freeway connects Verona to Vicenza, Padua and Venice. Central Verona is a ZTL (Limited Traffic Zone), though visitors are permitted to drive within the zone to drop off luggage at their hotel. Consider spending at least one night (*see* p. 151). Like any good lover, Verona will make it worth your while.

→ Appetising offerings at Salumeria Caliari Manuel

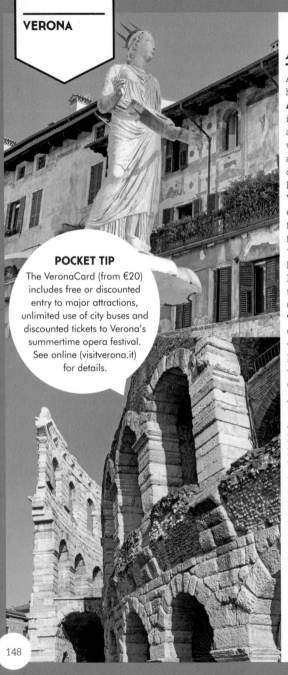

POCKET TIP

The VeronaCard (from €20)
includes free or discounted
entry to major attractions,
unlimited use of city buses and
discounted tickets to Verona's
summertime opera festival.
See online (visitverona.it)
for details.

SIGHTS

An archaeological meteor
hurled in from 30 CE, the
Arena di Verona (Piazza Brà)
is one of the best-preserved
ancient amphitheatres in the
world. In the summer, it's also
an evocative setting for top-tier
opera and concerts (arena.it).
From the arena, boutique-lined
Via Mazzini leads towards
elegant **Piazza delle Erbe**,
former site of Verona's Roman
forum. Topping the square's
14th-century fountain is a
late 4th-century statue of the
Madonna Verona. Looming to
the north, the 84 metre-high
(275-foot) medieval watchtower
Torre dei Lamberti (Via della
Costa 1) offers drone-worthy
views of Verona's rooftops and
hills. Opt for a combination
ticket to roam the adjoining
**Galleria d'Arte Moderna
Achille Forti**, home to
19th- and early 20th-century
artworks from prolific names
like Francesco Hayez, Umberto
Boccioni and Giorgio Morandi.
While you'd be forgiven for
wanting to glimpse the nearby
Casa di Giulietta (Juliet's
balcony, Via Cappello 23),
I suggest leaving it to the
hordes and instead crossing
the Adige River to the infinitely
more romantic **Giardino
Giusti** (Via Giardino Giusti 2),
a Renaissance garden with
enchanting views.

POCKET TIP
If it's the first Sunday of the month (August excluded), scrounge around at the always-fun flea market Verona Antiquaria (Piazza San Zeno).

SHOPPING

Tucked away on a side street between the Arena di Verona (*see* p. 148) and Verona Porta Nuova train station, **Libreria Antiquaria Perini** (Via Sciesa 11) is a trove of unique vintage prints and books, from 16th-century botanical illustrations and maps, to retro advertising. The store has furnished a number of film sets, including *Call Me by Your Name*, and sibling co-owners Alberto and Marcus are always happy to show off some of the more unusual items in stock. Prices range from serious collector to rookie. At neighbouring **Fil Good** (Via Sciesa 3c), designers Laura and Gloria hand make leather goods like bags and natural-fibre threads, designed with comfort and a simple, boho-chic vibe in mind. Impeccably stylish bags, wallets, belts and office accessories for both women and men await at **Cordovano** (Piazzetta Scala 2), the workshop-cum-showroom of master craftsman Mario Gastaldin.

149

EATING & DRINKING

Home of pandoro (a yeasty Christmas cake), Verona has a robust culinary scene. Prime produce and modern creativity inspire linen-clad **Locanda 4 Cuochi** (Via Alberto Mario 12), where memorable dishes look like playful modern artworks but book ahead (045 803 0311). For a cheap, satisfying bite to go, grab a porchetta sandwich from **Salumeria Caliari Manuel** (Corso Sant'Anastasia 33), a deli jammed with picnic-hamper treats, including salame di Verona all'Amarone (salami infused with Amarone wine).

To sample the area's world-famous vino, swill at **Antica Bottega del Vino** (Vicolo Scudo di Francia 3), a woody wine bar with an outstanding selection of wines by the glass, including an entire blackboard dedicated to Amarone. The rear dining room (book online at least three days ahead; bottegavini.it) is famous for its risotto all'Amarone (Amarone-wine risotto), though budget-conscious gourmands should stick to the decent front-bar cicheti (Venetian tapas).

For pastries and dolci (cakes), loosen your belt at **Pasticceria Flego** (Via Stella 13).

POCKET TIP

For an adrenalin-pumping overview of the city, Adige Rafting runs super-fun rafting adventures along the Adige River. In summer, combined rafting-and-aperitivo tours are usually available; book ahead (adigerafting.it).

✓LEEPING

Verona merits a sleepover, with no shortage of atmospheric hotels, B&Bs and apartment rentals in the city centre. If you feel like spoiling yourself, crash at **Palazzo Monga Boutique Guesthouse** (Corso Porta Borsari 36). Set in an 18th-century palazzo, it has a knack for balancing antique paintings and period furniture with contemporary soaking tubs and luxe amenities. The property includes a small gym, perfect for offloading excess carbs.

Directly opposite medieval fortress Castelvecchio is the surprisingly affordable, four-room **Il Relais** (Corso Castelvecchio 23), graced with heirloom furniture, objets d'art and bathrooms clad in local red marble. Food lovers will appreciate its in-house restaurant **Locanda Castelvecchio**, renowned for its regional cooking.

For a more rural experience, bunker down at budget-friendly **Corte San Mattia** (Via Santa Giuliana 2a), around 2.5 kilometres (1.5 miles) north of central Verona. An atmospheric agriturismo (farm stay) surrounded by olive groves, vineyards and orchards, it too has a reputable restaurant, paired with beautiful views of Verona itself.

GETTING TO VENICE

From Venice Marco Polo Airport

Located 13 kilometres (8 miles) from Piazzale Roma in Venice, Venice Marco Polo (VCE) is the city's main airport. Year-round destinations include cities in Italy and the rest of Europe, as well as a handful of destinations in the Middle East and Asia. Seasonal routes include the USA and Canada. The airport is easily accessible from the city.

Boat Shuttle

Aliguna Airport Shuttle (alilaguna.it) runs three routes (blue, orange, red) to various parts of Venice. Travel time is between 45 to 90 minutes. A one-way ticket is €8 to Murano and €15 to all other stops, including Rialto, San Marco and Arsenale. The price includes one suitcase and one piece of hand luggage; extra luggage is €3 per piece. Return and online tickets are slightly cheaper.

Water Taxi

Consorzio Motoscafi Venezia (motoscafivenezia.it) and Venezia Taxi (veneziataxi.it) run private water taxis between the airport and Venice. Trips cost from €115 for up to four or five passengers and luggage. Extra passengers carry a surcharge.

Venice Shuttle (venicelink.com) operates a shared water-taxi service carrying eight to 12 passengers. Cost per person is from €22, plus a €10 surcharge for night-time arrivals. Venice Shuttle boats serve set drop-off points. Book at least 24 hours ahead.

Taxi

Taxis between the airport and Piazzale Roma cost €40. The fare is valid for up to four passengers, including luggage. Travel time takes around 20 minutes, subject to traffic. See online (radiotaxivenezia.com).

Bus

ACTV (actv.avmspa.it) bus line 5 (Aerobus) runs between the airport and Piazzale Roma (€8; around 30 minutes). A combined Aerobus+Boat ticket (€14) is valid for 90 minutes and includes one vaporetto (ferry) trip in Venice. ATVO (atvo.it) line 25 also runs to Piazzale Roma (€8).

From Treviso Airport

Located 32 kilometres (20 miles) north of Piazzale Roma, Treviso Airport (TSF) services low-cost European carriers Ryanair and Wizzair, with flights to numerous Italian and other European cities.

Bus

Barzi Bus Service (barziservice.com) runs buses between Treviso Airport and Tronchetto (Venice), from where a monorail continues to Piazzale Roma. Tickets are €12, with a journey time around 40 minutes. ATVO runs buses to Mestre and Piazzale Roma (€12).

Train

Treviso AirLink (mobilitadimarca.it) shuttle buses connect to Treviso train station (€3.50; 15 minutes), from where trains continue to Venice's train station, Venezia Santa Lucia (€3.60; 30 to 40 minutes).

Taxi

Taxis (taxitreviso.it) between Treviso Airport and Venice cost €76 for up to four passengers, including luggage but excluding Sunday and nighttime surcharges. The trip time is 45 and 60 minutes, subject to traffic.

GETTING AROUND VENICE

On Foot

The best way to explore the city is by walking. Remember to walk on the right, especially in narrower calli (streets). Be mindful of slippery footbridges and canal banks on wet days.

Vaporetto

ACTV-run city vaporetti (ferries) sail along main canals, with numerous handy stops on both the Grand and Giudecca Canals. These include Piazzale Roma (airport buses), Ferrovia (Venezia Santa Lucia train station), Rialto (Rialto Bridge), Accademia (Gallerie dell'Accademia), Salute (Basilica di Santa Maria della Salute, Peggy Guggenheim

Collection), San Marco (Basilica di San Marco, Palazzo Ducale and Museo Correr) and San Giorgio (Isola di San Giorgio Maggiore). They also reach islands further afield, among them Murano, Burano, Torcello and the Lido di Venezia. You'll find well-marked route maps at vaporetto (ferry) stops.

Single tickets (€7.50) are valid for 75 minutes. Day and multiday passes (1/2/3/7 days, €20/30/40/60) also available. Purchase them from ACTV ticket booths and vending machines at ferry stops or from tobacconists.

Each passenger can carry three pieces of luggage free of charge, provided that one piece does not exceed a combined length, width and height of 150cm (60 inches) while the other two pieces do not exceed a combined length and width and height of 120cm (47 inches) each. Extra luggage will require a ticket. See online (actv.avmspa.it/en) for details.

Traghetto
Popular with locals, traghetti are affordable daytime public gondolas that cross the Grand Canal at various points between the canal's four bridges. Single ticket €2.

Gondola
Thirty-minute rides cost €80 (maximum of six passengers) between 7am and 7pm and usually take you through smaller canals and out onto the Grand Canal. There are specific gondola stops ('Servizio Gondole' or 'Gondola') or you can ask a gondolier to take you from anywhere. Between 7pm and 3am, 35-minute rides cost €100. Rates exclude songs (negotiated separately) and tips.

Water Taxi
Water taxis charge €15 followed by an additional €2 per minute. Numerous surcharges include for luggage, pre-booked services and night trips. Pick-up points include Piazzale Roma, Ferrovia (Venezia Santa Lucia train station), and by the Ponte di Rialto (Rialto Bridge). Ensure the meter is working when boarding.

TIME ZONES

Venice – like the rest of Italy – lies in the Western European time zone (GMT/UTC plus one hour). Clocks go forward one hour during daylight savings, which runs from the last Sunday in March to the last Sunday in October.

TOURIST INFORMATION

Official tourist association Vènezia Unica (veneziaunica.it) operates information kiosks at numerous locations. These include Venice Marco Polo Airport, Piazzale Roma, Ferrovia (Venezia Santa Lucia train station) and Piazza San Marco.

MONEY & ATMS

Italy's currency is the euro, denoted by €. Euro coins come in denominations of €1 and €2, as well as one, two, five, 10, 20 and 50 cents. Euro notes come in denominations of €5, €10, €20, €50, €100, €200 and €500.

ATMs (called bancomat) are common in Venice and most accept international cards. Major credit cards are widely accepted, although some smaller and/or more traditional trattorias and shops may only accept cash.

TIPPING

Although Italy does not have a strong tipping culture, consider tipping 10% of the total bill if servizio (service) is not included in restaurants. In coffee bars, most locals leave a €0.10 or €0.20 coin on the counter for the barista. For cocktails, a €1 to €2 tip per drink is considered gracious. Porters at higher-end hotels should be tipped about €5. Round off taxi fares to the nearest euro. A discretionary tip of between €5 and €10 is common for gondoliers.

TAX

A 22% IVA (value-added tax) is included in the price of most goods and services. Accommodation is subject to a tassa di soggiorno (room-occupancy tax), charged on top of your bill. The rate per person per night ranges from around €1 to €5 and is applicable for a maximum of five consecutive nights.

The Venice City Council's controversial contributo di accesso (access fee) is planned to be fully implemented from 2022. Aimed at tourists visiting the city as a daytrip only, the tax will cost between €3 and €10, with peak period tourists charged highest. Veneto region residents, travellers with disabilities and children under age six are among those expected to be exempt from the fee.

CLIMATE

Venice has a humid sub-tropical climate. Mild weather and thinning crowds make autumn the best time to visit. Spring is usually damp while summer can be uncomfortably humid, hot and crowded. Many businesses close in August when Italians take their annual leave. Winter days are chilly, though snow is rare.

PHONES

Venice's area code is 041. Always dial the code, even when calling local numbers. To avoid high roaming charges, consider buying an Italian SIM prepagata (prepaid SIM card), available from Italian telco stores for TIM (tim.it), Wind (wind.it), Vodafone (vodafone.it) and Tre (tre.it). You will need your passport or ID card when buying a local SIM card. Do not buy SIM cards at the airport, as they generally offer less competitive deals.

WI-FI

Free wi-fi is available at many cafes and bars, as well as in most hotels, B&Bs and rental apartments. You can also buy access to city wi-fi hotspots (24/72 hours €5/15, 7 days €20) through Venezia Unica (veneziaunica.it).

ETIQUETTE

Venice is a photographer's dream but whether taking photos or checking Google Maps, don't block streets and bridges; they're treated like roads by locals. Cover shoulders and knees when visiting religious sites and don't wear flip-flops to restaurants. Walking around the city shirtless or in swimwear can land you a fine.

If invited to a Venetian home for lunch or dinner, take a bottle of wine or a vassoio di paste (tray of pastries) from a local pasticerria (patisserie).

NAVIGATIONAL DISCREPANCIES

Venice is enigmatic right down to its thoroughfares. Some streets and squares are known by more than one name, while some streets change name several times along their route. The spelling of street names and squares can also vary between maps, whether they're printed hotel maps or digital maps on your phone. While some opt for the Venetian name, others use official Italian. For ease of navigation, the addresses given in this guidebook mainly reflect the names of the streets and squares as they appear on the actual street signs.

LGBTIAQ+ TRAVELLERS

Homosexuality is legal in Italy and generally accepted in Venice, especially among younger generations. That said, the city is low on LGBTIAQ+-specific venues, with mixed crowds common at bars. For more queer-specific nightlife, head to Padua (*see* p. 134).

SHOPPING TIPS

If you are a non-EU resident and spend over €155 at one shop with a Tax Free sign, you are eligible for a refund when leaving the EU. You will need to ask the shop assistant for a tax-refund voucher, which needs to be filled in with the date of purchase and value. When leaving the EU, have the voucher stamped at the airport tax-refund counter or by customs. The refund can be made in cash or transferred to your credit card. For details, see online (taxrefund.it).

Most shops accept credit cards, though some smaller businesses and most market vendors will only accept cash. Good-natured haggling is generally only accepted at flea markets.

Most importantly, always consider ditching cheap, foreign-made souvenirs and clothes for locally made wares; such as those showcased in this guide. This ensures you help sustain local jobs and lives.

SUSTAINABLE VENICE

Venice's ongoing battle against unsustainable tourism has made world headlines in recent years, from the environmental concerns surrounding cruise ships to the overcrowding and littering attributed in part to daytrippers. To enjoy the city more sustainably, avoid visiting in the peak seasons, especially Carnevale season (Jan/Feb; varies) and summer. October is still relatively mild, while January fog accentuates the brooding, Gothic beauty of the city. Avoiding peak season also means fewer crowds and cheaper accommodation.

When booking a place, consider staying in a proper B&B or hotel to support local jobs. If you prefer renting your own pad, find a place through Fairbnb (fairbnb.coop), an ethical home-sharing site that supports local residents and donates 50 per cent of its own commission to community projects. At the Mercato di Rialto (see p. 40), seek out produce labelled nostrano (locally grown or caught) and always opt for a reusable water bottle; the local tap water is perfectly drinkable. Online, check out Venezia Autentica (veneziaautentica.com), which lists eateries, bars, shops and services that support a sustainable local economy.

SAFETY

Venice is generally very safe, though petty crimes exists. Always keep your bags closed and in sight and never store wallets and valuables in easy-to-reach pockets. In case of theft or loss, report the incident to the police (either the Polizia or Carabinieri) within 24 hours and request a statement.

If you find yourself in an emergency, dial 112 or 113 for police, 115 for the fire brigade or 118 for urgent medical assistance.

Foreign embassies are based in Rome, though numerous countries – including Australia, New Zealand, the UK, USA and Canada – also have a consulate in Milan.

OPENING HOURS

Opening hours can vary significantly in Venice (and Italy in general). Many cultural attractions and businesses operate seasonal times, with extended opening hours from around April to late October. Churches often close for an hour or so at lunch and some smaller businesses may wrap up earlier than their official closing time if business is especially slow on a particular day. The recent Covid-19 pandemic has only added to the changeability of trading hours at many shops, restaurants and bars. Consequently, opening times are not listed in this guidebook, with readers encouraged to check the latest opening times online.

TOILETS

If you're out and nature calls, your easiest bet is to pop into a cafe or bar (though you should always purchase something as a courtesy). Toilets are common at museums and major department stores, including Fondaco dei Tedeschi, located steps from Ponte di Rialto (Rialto Bridge).

The free-to-download Bagni a Venezia (Restrooms in Venice; wctoilettevenezia. com) app maps public toilets (€1.50) across the city, all suitable for people with limited mobility.

VENETIAN FOOD

Given Venice's coastal setting, it's not surprising that fresh fish and seafood feature prominently on local menus. The list of food and dishes here will help you navigate eating like a Venetian.

aceto (vinegar)
alla mescita (by the glass)
allergia (allergy)
antipasto di pesce (seafood antipasto)
aperitivo (aperitif)
arancini (fried rice balls)
asparagi bianchi di Bassano (Bassano white asparagus)
assaggio (a tasting/tasting plate)
baccalà (stockfish or salted cod)
baccalà mantecato (creamed salted cod)
bigoli in salsa (thick spaghetti with anchovy-and-onion sauce)
biologico/bio (organic)
birra (beer)
birra alla spina (tap beer)
bottiglia (bottle)
brindisi (toast)
bussolai buranelli (Burano butter biscuits)
busta (shopping bag)
caffè (coffee)
carciofi (artichokes)
carne (meat)
carpaccio (thinly sliced raw meat)
carta dei vini (wine list)
castraure (violet baby artichokes)
cicheti (Venetian tapas)
condimenti (condiments)
crostini (small open-faced sandwiches)
crudo (raw fish)
crostoli/galani (crunchy, deep-fried pastry ribbons dusted in icing sugar)
digestivo (digestif)
dolce (sweet/dessert)
fegato alla veneziana (Venetian-style calf livers with simmered onions)
fiori di zucca (zucchini flowers)
formaggio (cheese)
fritòle (rum-laced Venetian doughnuts with raisins)
frutta (fruit)
frutti di mare (seafood)
gamberoni (large prawns)
ghiaccio (ice)
gnocchetti (small gnocchi)
il conto (the bill/check)

mezza porzione (half portion)
moeche (small, local, soft-shell crabs)
noci (nuts)
nostrano (locally caught/grown)
ombra (small glass of wine)
orzo (a hot barley drink)
pancetta coppata in saor (salt-cured pork belly in a sweet-and-sour sauce)
pandoro (yeasty, star-shaped Christmas cake)
pane (bread)
paninetti (small sandwiches)
pasta e fagioli (dense pasta soup with beans)
pastine (bite-sized pastries)
pesce (fish)
piccante (spicy)
pizza al taglio (pizza by the slice)
polenta e schie (small local shrimps served on polenta)
polpette (meatballs)
primo (first course)
radicchio rosso di Treviso (mildly bitter Treviso chicory)
risi e bisi (thick soup of rice, peas and pancetta)
riso (rice)
risotto di gò (risotto with goby fish)
sale e pepe (salt and pepper)
salsicce (sausages)
salumi (cured meats)
sarde in saor (sweet-and-sour sardines)
scampi e calamari fritti (fried langoustine and calamari)
secondo (second/main course)
senza glutine (gluten free)
seppie alla veneziana (squid-ink cuttlefish with polenta)
spaghetti alla busara (spaghetti with langoustine, tomato, chilli and parsley)
speck (cured, slightly smoked ham)
spiedini (skewers)
taglieri (platters)
tè (tea)
tisane (herbal teas)
tramezzini (mini sandwiches)
uova (eggs)
vegano (vegan)
vegeteriano (vegetarian)
verdura (vegetables)
vino naturale (natural wine)
zabaione (marsala-infused cream)
zuppa di pesce (fish soup)
zuppa di trippa (tripe soup)
zucchero (sugar)

CICHETI

The most unique aspect of the local food scene is arguably cicheti (pronounced chee-KET-ee). Venice's answer to Spanish tapas, these morsels are readily available at bacarì, wine bars known for offering ombre (small glasses of wine) and graze-friendly small plates. In truth, cicheti span a wide range of options, from toothpick-speared polpette (meatballs) and olive ascolane (deep-fried stuffed olives), to pancetta-wrapped local shrimps. Crostini (small open-faced sandwiches) are especially popular, topped with anything from classic baccala mantecato to creative combos like brie and stinging nettles, or salmon and mascarpone. While individual cicheti can cost anything from €1 to around €6, depending on the ingredients, most average around €1.50 to €2. Six to eight usually make a meal, making cicheti a fantastic meal for budget-conscious food lovers. Tip: Head in early (around noon at lunch, 6pm in the evening) for the best selection.

HOLIDAY/

Most Italians take their annual leave in August, when many escape al mare (to the beach) or in montagna (to the mountains). As a result, some shops and restaurants in Venice close for a few weeks during this month. Official public holidays are:

Capodanno (New Year's Day) 1 January
Epifania (Epiphany) 6 January
Pasquetta (Easter Monday) March/April
Giorno della Liberazione (Liberation Day) 25 April
Festa del Lavoro (Labour Day) 1 May
Festa della Repubblica (Republic Day) 2 June
Festa dei Santi Pietro e Paolo (Feast of St Peter & St Paul) 29 June
Ferragosto (Feast of the Assumption) 15 August
Ognisanti (All Saints' Day) 1 November
Immacolata Concezione (Feast of the Immaculate Conception) 8 December
Natale (Christmas Day) 25 December
Festa di Santo Stefano (Boxing Day) 26 December

DRINKING IN VENICE

Venetians love a tipple and the Veneto region claims some of Italy's most famous libations, including sparkling prosecco. The finest – Prosecco Superiore DOCG – hails from the hills between Conegliano and Valdobiaddene north of Venice. Prosecco and pureed white peaches make a classic Venetian Bellini cocktail, while prosecco, soda water and Aperol make an Aperol spritz. For a more herbaceous spritz, swap the Aperol for Cynar, an Italian bitter made with artichoke. The hills between Vicenza and Verona produce seafood-friendly Soave – a white wine made with Veneto Garganega grapes – while the Valpolicella wine region north of Verona is lauded for a string of reds. These include easy-drinking Valpolicella, the more structured DOC Valpolicella Ripasso and the daddy of all Veneto reds – rich, deep, intense Amarone. The Veneto is also known for grappa, produced in a variety of smooth, nuanced versions, including barricata, which is aged in French oak barrels.

On the coffee front, most locals only drink cappuccino or caffè latte in the morning. From midday, espresso is the coffee of choice. An espresso is simply called un caffè. Order a latte and you'll get a glass of milk. You will need to specify caffè latte. Never order a coffee with your lunch or dinner; only after.

FESTIVALS & EVENTS

Venice claims some spectacular festivals. Top annual events include the following:

Carnevale (Jan/Feb) The two weeks preceding Lent are marked by masks, elaborate costumes, parades, parties and huge crowds in a tradition reputedly dating back to the mid-12th century. Book accommodation well in advance.

La Biennale di Venezia (May–Nov) An A-list international arts festival, alternating between contemporary art (odd-numbered years) and architecture (even-numbered years). The Biennale also incorporates the annual Venice Film Festival.

Vogalonga (May/Jun) Around 2000 boats and over 7000 rowers from Italy and beyond take part in this 32 kilometre (20 mile) rowing regatta from Palazzo Ducale to Punta della Dogana, held on Whitsunday.

Regatta Storica (Sept) Period costumes and elaborate barques define this Grand Canal rowing race, its history spanning back to the mid-13th century.

USEFUL WORDS & PHRASES

While it is easy enough to get by with English in Venice, knowing some basic Italian words and phrases is handy and a good way to charm the locals.

Hello: Ciao (informal)/ Salve (polite)
Goodbye: Arrivederci
Good morning: Buongiorno
Good evening: Buona sera
Good night: Buona notte
How are you?: Come stai? (informal)/ Come sta? (polite)
I'm well, thanks: Sto bene, grazie
Do you speak English?: Parla inglese?
I don't understand: Non capisco
Nice to meet you: Molto lieto
Please: Per piacere/per favore
Thank you: Grazie
Thank you very much: Grazie mille
Excuse me: Scusi
May I?: Posso?
How much is this: Quanto costa?
Cheers!: Salute!/Cin cin!
Delicious: Buonissimo!
I'm full: Sono sazio (male)/sono sazia (female)
Can I have the bill please?: Il conto, per favore
Airport: Aeroporto
Station: Stazione
Train: Treno
Bus: Autobus
Public ferry: Vaporetto
Where do I need to get off?: Dove devo scendere?
I love Venice/Italy!: Amo Venezia/l'Italia!

MURANO

Laguna   Veneta

180–1

CANNAREGIO
176–7

ISOLA DI
SAN MICHELE

170

178–9

168–9
SAN
POLO

166–7

SANTA
CROCE

CASTELLO

171

SAN
MARCO
173

162–3

164–5

DORSODURO

172

182

Sant'Elena

GIUDECCA

174–5

La Grazia

Isola di
San Sèrvolo

B
C
①
②
③
④
A
B
C

VENICE

Isola
Buel del Lovo

183   TORCELLO

MAZZORBO   BURANO

Isola Carbonera

Isola della
Madonna
del Monte

Laguna   *Veneta*

Isola di
San Francesco
del Deserto

Isola di Tessera

Isola di
San Giacomo
in Paludo

MURANO

Lazzaretto
Nuovo

Isola di Sant'Erasmo

ISOLA DI
SAN MICHELE

Vignole

SAN
MARCO   CASTELLO

Sant'Elena

ISOLA DI
SAN GIORGIO
MAGGIORE

Lido di Venezia

Isola di
San Sèrvolo

Isola di
San Clemente

Spadaria

Ponte dei
Consorzi

Calle del Figher

San Marco

C. Rimpeto la Sacrestia

Larga

Virtuosi di
Venezia
(San Marco
Chamber
Orchestra)

Calle de la Canonica

Ponte
Cappello

Campo Santi
Filippo e Giacomo

Calle
Marzaria dell'Orologio

Ponte de la
Canonica

Museo Diocesano
di Venezia

Calle dei Albanesi

Calle de le Rasse

**BASILICA
DI SAN
MARCO**

Rio   de   Palazzo

Campanile di San Marco
(bell tower)

Calle   dei   Albanesi

Calle   de   le   Rasse

**PALAZZO
DUCALE**

Ponte dei
Sospiri
(Bridge of Sighs)

⊕ **MUSEO
ARCHEOLOGICO
NAZIONALE
DI VENEZIA**

Riva   degli   Schiavoni

⊕ **BIBLIOTECA
NAZIONALE
MARCIANA**

Ponte
della
Paglia

Colonna di
San Marco

Colonna di
San Teodoro

3

Molo   di   Palazzo   Ducale

San Marco
(San Zaccaria)

🚣 **Gondola
station**

Bacino di San Marco

⊿
N

0   50 m

Giardino
dell'Ordine
di Malta

**Chiesa di
San Giovanni
di Malta**

Calle Dona

Ternita

Calle Malatin

Calle Drasi

Calle

Salizada de le Gare

Rio dei Scudi Santa

Calle

Magno

Calle de l'Anzolo

Campo
delle
Gate

Ponte
dei Scudi

Calle dei Furlani

CASTELLO

Calle dei Scudi

Calle del Forno

C. de le Muneghere

Rio de le Gorne

**Chiesa di
Sant'Antonin**

BANCO
LOTTO N.10

del'Arco

Calle del San Martin

Piscina San Martin

Calle del Bastion

⊕ 2

Salizada San Antonin

Calle

Ponte
della
Grana

Campiello
della Grana

ATELIER
ALESSANDRO
MERLIN

Canale delle Galeazze

Calle della Morte

Salizada

Delpignater

Pestrin

ARSENALE

Rio dell'Arsenale

⊕

**Campo
Bandiera
e Moro**

**CHIESA
DI SAN
GIOVANNI
IN BRAGORA**
⊕

Calle del

Calle Gritti

Calle drio Erizzo

Ponte
Sorto

Fondamenta de Fazza l'Arsenal

Calle de l'Arsenal

Fondamenta del Piovan

**CHIESA
DI SAN
MARTINO**
⊕

Calle Streta

Calle Larga

**Campo de
l'Arsenal**

Ponte de
l'Arsenal o
del Paradiso

⊕ 3

Campiello del Piovan

Calle Erizzo

Calle Grandi

Ca' di Dio

de l'Arsenale

AL COVO
⊕

Calle del Forno

Calle de la Pescaria

Calle Morosina

Rio della

Calle del Forni

Calle de la Vida

Rio dell'Arsenale

Fondamenta

⊕ 4

Schiavoni

Ponte della
Ca' di Dio

Riva de

Ca' di Dio

Bacino di San Marco

D E F

I

Calle de la Testa

Rio dei Mendicanti
Fondamenta dei Mendicanti

N

0   50 m

Scuola Grande
di San Marco

Chiesa di
Santa Maria
del Pianto

BASILICA DEI
SS GIOVANNI
E PAOLO
(SAN ZANIPOLO)

Campo
Santi
Giovanni
e Paolo

Calle Torelli detta de la Cavalerizza

Chiesa di
Santa Maria
dei Derelitti

Calle Nicolo Massa

2

Barbaria

de le   Tole

C. de le Moschete

GIBRAN

Calle del Cafetier

Pestrin

Calle Trevisana o Cicogna

Ponte dei
Conzafelzi

LIBRERIA
ACQUA
ALTA

Rio de San Giovanni Laterano

Corte
Muazzo

Corte
de le
Do Porte

Calle

Calle Schiavolina

Cocco

Santa Maria

Formosa

Rio de la Tetta

Campiello
Cappello

3

Campo
nta Maria
ormosa

Calle Longa Santa Maria

Formosa

CASTELLO

Chiesa di
San Lorenzo

Chiesa di
Santa Maria
Formosa

Maria

Museo di
Palazzo
Grimani

Calle Larga San Lorenzo

Campo
San Lorenzo

onte de
Bande

de Santa

Ruga

Ponte
Novo

Borgoloco San Lorenzo

Ponte de
San Lorenzo

Rio

Calle de Mezo

Rio de San Severo

Fondamenta San Lorenzo

Rio di San Lorenzo

Fondazione
Querini
Stampalia
(museum)

Giuffa

Calle de l'Arco

Fondamenta San Severo

4

C. Querini Stampalia

Salizada Zorzi

Campo
San
Severo

Calle dei Preti

Ponte
Lion

Calle   Lion

D E F

OSTERIA LA ZUCCA

CA' PESARO

Calle Langa

Calle dei Tentor

Calle del Forno

Salizada San Stae

Rio de Ca' Tron

Ramo Terzo Carminati

Fondamenta Rimpeto Mocenigo

GELATO DI NATURA

Calle Colombo

Boldo

MUSEO DI PALAZZO MOCENIGO

Carminati

Chiesa di San Giacomo dall'Orio

Rio de San

Salizada

San Stae

SANTA CROCE

Calle de Mezo

Rio de la Pergola o de Ca Pesaro

Chiesa di Santa Maria Mater Domini

RISTORANTE REGINA SCONTA

OSTERIA DA FILO

Ponte Storto

Rio

Calle del Modena

Campo Santa Maria Mater Domini

Longa

Rio de Santa Maria Mater Domini

Calle de la Regina

Campo San Boldo

Rio de San Giacomo dell'Orio

Rio Terà Primo del Parucheta

N

0   50 m

PAPEROOWL

Calle

Calle de l'Agnella

C. del Filosi

Secondo

Calle del Scaleter

Calle del Cristo

C. de la Comedia

Rio Terà

Rio San Cassian

Calle del Pistor

Calle Cà Bernardo

Campiello Sant'Agostin

Ponte Ca' Donà

Rio de le Do Torre

Calle

Pezzana

Campiello Albrizzi

Calle Tamos

Calle de Cà Corner

Calle Streta

Sant'Aponal

Rio de San Stin

Rio

San

Polo

Palazzo Corner Mocenigo

Palazzo Soranzo

Rio

Rio dei Melon

Calle del Albanesi

Calle del Forno

Corte Amaltea

Campo San Polo

PASTICCERIA RIZZARDINI

Campiello dei Meloni

Chiesa di San Polo

A   B   C

GALLERIA GIORGIO FRANCHETTI ALLA CA' D'ORO

Chiesa di Santa Sofia

FEELIN' VENICE

Canal

Ca' d'Oro

Calle del Forno

Calle de l'Oca

Calle de la Pegola

Ca' Corner della Regina

Calle de Ca' Corner

Calle del Rosa

Rio San Cassian

Grande

Fondamenta Riva de l'Ogio

Chiesa di San Cassiano

Calle del Campaniel

Calle dei Boteri

MERCATO DI RIALTO

Rialto Mercato

Campo San Cassian

C. de l'Erbariol

Calle dei Cristi

Calle de le Becarie

Campo de le Becarie

Calle de la Campana

Calle de l'Ostaria de la Campana

C. Prima de la Donzella

Calle de la Donzella

Calle Drio la Scimia

Calle de la Scimia

Campo Cesare Battisti già della Bella Vienna

Calle de Ca' Muti

Calle dei Boteri

Calle de la Bota

Rio de le Becarie

Calle Riveta

CANTINA DO MORI

CASA DEL PARMIGIANO

Ruga dei Oresi

Campo Erbaria

ALL'ARCO

Campiello dei Sansoni

Calle San Giovanni

Sotoportego

Chiesa di San Giacomo Apostolo

Campiello del Sol

Ponte Storto

Ruga Vecchia

Calle de la

CAFFÈ DEL DOGE

Campo Rialto Novo

de Rialto

PONTE DI RIALTO

Chiesa di Sant'Aponal

Ravano

Rugheta del

Calle dei Cinque

Calle del Paradiso

Calle dei Sturion

Madona

Vin

Grande

Campo Sant' Aponal

SAN POLO

Riva

del

Calle de Mezo

C. del Luganegher

Calle dei Sbanchesini

Calle Dolera

Campo de San Silvestro

Chiesa di San Silvestro

Rialto

Canal

D   E   F

1

2

3

4

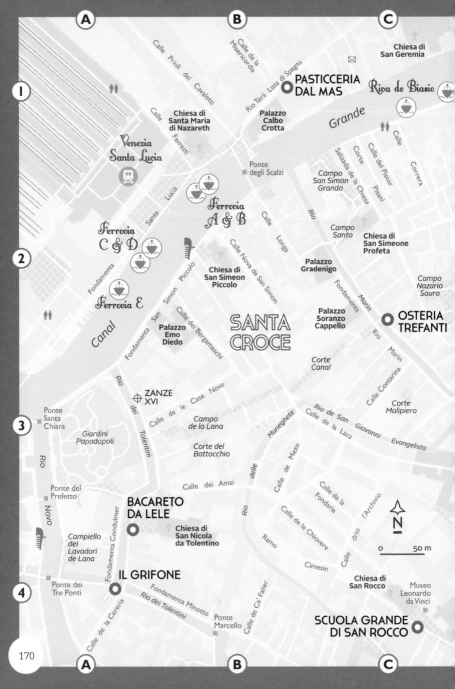

A

Chiesa di Santa Maria di Nazareth

Venezia Santa Lucia

Ferrovia C & D

Ferrovia E

Canal

Ponte Santa Chiara

Giardini Papadopoli

Ponte del Prefetto

Campiello dei Lavadori de Lana

Ponte dei Tre Ponti

B

Calle Priuli dei Cavaletti

Calle de la Misericordia

Calle Favretti

Santa Lucia

PASTICCERIA DAL MAS

Rio Terà Lista di Spagna

Palazzo Calbo Crotta

Ponte degli Scalzi

Ferrovia A & B

Calle Nova de San Simon

Calle Longa

Chiesa di San Simeon Piccolo

Fondamenta San Simon Piccolo

Calle del Bergamaschi

Palazzo Emo Diedo

SANTA CROCE

⊕ **ZANZE XVI**

Rio dei Tolentini

Calle de le Case Nove

Campo de la Lana

Corte del Battocchio

Calle dei Amai

BACARETO DA LELE

Fondamenta Condulmer

Chiesa di San Nicola da Tolentino

IL GRIFONE

Fondamenta Minotto

Calle de la Cereria

Rio dei Tolentini

Rio de le Muneghete

Calle de la Laca

Rio delle Muneghete

Calle de Mezo

Rio

Ramo

Calle de le Chiovere

Calle de la Fondaria

Ponte Marcello

Calle de Ca' Falier

C

Chiesa di San Geremia

Grande

Riva de Biasio

Salizada de la Chiesa

Corte Pisani

Calle del Pistor

Calle

Correra

Campo San Simon Grando

Campo Santo

Chiesa di San Simeone Profeta

Palazzo Gradenigo

Campo Nazario Sauro

Fondamenta Marin

Palazzo Soranzo Cappello

OSTERIA TREFANTI

Rio Marin

Corte Canal

Calle Contarina

Corte Malipiero

Rio de San Giovanni Evangelista

Calle drio l'Archivio

Chiesa di San Rocco

Museo Leonardo da Vinci

SCUOLA GRANDE DI SAN ROCCO

N

0   50 m

A B C

SCUOLA GRANDE
DI SAN GIOVANNI
EVANGELISTA

PALAZZETTO
BRU ZANE

Calle de la Laca

Calle drio l'Archivio

Calle de Mezo

Calle de la Laca

Calle de

Calle del Campazzo

Calle de la Fondaria

Calle drio l'Archivio

Calle de la Vida

Calle Donà o del Spezier

1

Chiesa di
San Giovanni
Evangelista

Calle de le Chiovere

Calle drio l'Archivio

Rio Terà
San Tomà

Calle del Magazen

Ramo Cimesin

Calle

0   50 m

SAN
POLO

PROCESS
COLLETTIVO

Rio

delle

Muneghete

Chiesa di
San Rocco

Museo
Leonardo da Vinci

BASILICA
DEI FRARI

IL MERCANTE

Rio dei Frari

2

Calle de Castelforte

SCUOLA
GRANDE DI
SAN ROCCO

Campo
San Rocco

LEGATORIO
POLLIERO
VENEZIA

Calle Nova

Corte Nova

Campo de
Castelforte

Campiello
San
Rocco

Calle dei Albanesi

Calle del Cristo

Calle Molin

Salizada
San Pantalon

MALVASIA
ALL'ADRIATICO
MAR

C. Gaspare Gozzi

Calle Stretta Lipoli

Campo
San
Tomà

Campiello
Mosca

ESTRO

Chiesa
di San
Tomà

PASTICCERIA
TONOLO

OHMYBLUE

3

Rio de San Pantalon

Chiesa di
San Pantalon

EL SBARLEFO

Calle San Pantalon

Calle

Gondola
station

BANKSY
MURAL

Calle

Rio de la Frescada

San Tomà

Ponte Santa
Margherita

Campo
San Pantalon

Crosera

Corte dei
Formacier

Calle de la Saonera

Rio de Ca' Foscari

Calle Larga Foscari

Calle Marcona

AI DO
DRAGHI

C. Salita Fontego

Palazzo
Balbi

Campo
Santa
Margherita

Corte
Marcona

Calle de la Saonera

Calle del Magazen

Ponte
Foscari

Canal

Grande

CAFFE
ROSSO

Calle de l'Aseo

PAOLO
OLBI

Ca'
Foscari

PIZZA AL VOLVO

Calle dei Saoneri

Calle Foscari

4

DORSODURO

Campiello
dei
Squelini

Palazzo
Giustinian

Calle   Bernardo

A B C

171

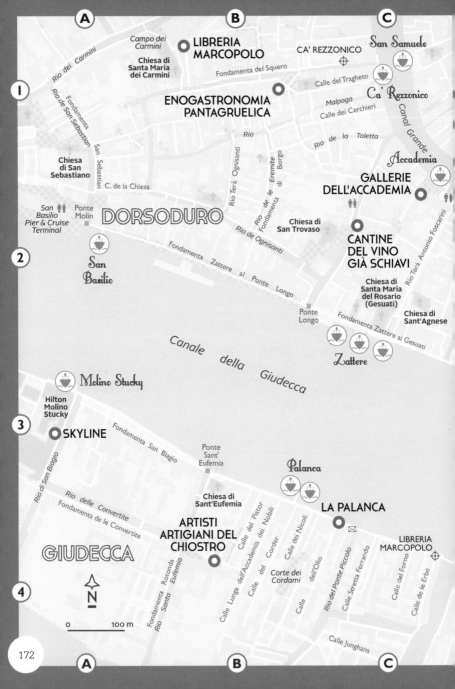

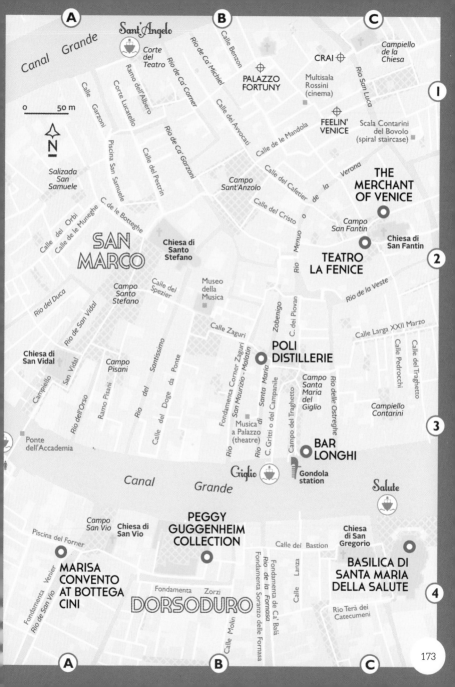

Canal Grande

A · B · C

Sant'Angelo

Corte del Teatro

Calle Benzon

Calle de Ca' Michiel

Rio de Ca' Corner

Ramo dell'Albero

Corte Lucatello

Calle Garzoni

Calle dei Avvocati

PALAZZO FORTUNY

CRAI

Campiello de la Chiesa

Multisala Rossini (cinema)

FEELIN' VENICE

Rio San Luca

1

o 50 m

N

Piscina San Samuele

Calle del Pestrin

Rio de Ca' Garzoni

Calle de la Mandola

Scala Contarini del Bovolo (spiral staircase)

Salizada San Samuele

Calle dei Orbi

Calle de le Muneghe

C. de le Botteghe

Campo Sant'Anzolo

Calle del Cafetier

Calle del Cristo

Verona

Calle del Cafetier de la

THE MERCHANT OF VENICE

SAN MARCO

Chiesa di Santo Stefano

Calle del Spezier

Museo della Musica

Rio Menuo

Campo San Fantin

Chiesa di San Fantin

TEATRO LA FENICE

2

Rio del Duca

Campo Santo Stefano

Rio de San Vidal

Calle Zaguri

Rio de la Veste

Chiesa di San Vidal

San Vidal

Campo Pisani

Ramo Pisani

Rio del Santissimo

Calle del Doge da Ponte

Fondamenta Corner Zaguri

San Maurizio – Malatin

Calle Gritti o del Campanile

Santa Maria

Zobenigo

C. dei Piovan

POLI DISTILLERIE

Campo Santa Maria del Giglio

Rio delle Ostreghe

Calle Larga XXII Marzo

Calle Pedrocchi

Calle del Traghetto

Campiello Contarini

3

Campiello

Rio dell'Orso

Ponte dell'Accademia

Rio

Musica a Palazzo (theatre)

Campo del Traghetto

BAR LONGHI

Giglio

Gondola station

Salute

Canal Grande

Campo San Vio

Chiesa di San Vio

PEGGY GUGGENHEIM COLLECTION

Calle del Bastion

Chiesa di San Gregorio

Piscina del Forner

Venier

Rio de San Vio

Fondamenta

MARISA CONVENTO AT BOTTEGA CINI

Fondamenta Zorzi

DORSODURO

Calle Molin

Fondamenta de Ca' Balà

Rio de la Fornasa

Fondamenta Soranzo delle Formasa

Calle Lanza

BASILICA DI SANTA MARIA DELLA SALUTE

Rio Terà dei Catecumeni

4

A · B · C

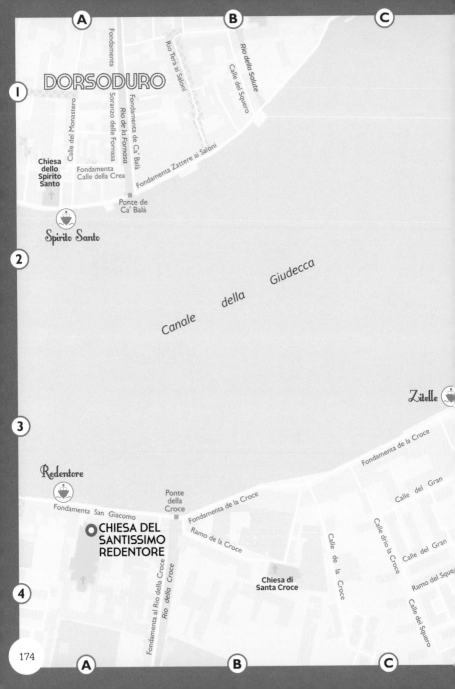

A · **B** · **C**

1

DORSODURO

Fondamenta

Rio Terà ai Saloni

Rio della Salute

Calle dello Squero

Calle del Monastero

Fondamenta

Soranzo delle Fornasa

Rio de la Fornasa

Fondamenta de Ca' Balà

Fondamenta

Calle della Crea

Fondamenta Zattere ai Saloni

Chiesa dello Spirito Santo

Ponte de Ca' Balà

Spirito Santo

2

Canale della Giudecca

3

Zitelle

Redentore

Fondamenta de la Croce

Fondamenta San Giacomo

Ponte della Croce

Fondamenta de la Croce

Calle del Gran

○ **CHIESA DEL SANTISSIMO REDENTORE**

Ramo de la Croce

Calle dro la Croce

Calle del Gran

Calle de la Croce

Ramo del Sque

Fondamenta al Rio della Croce

Rio della Croce

Chiesa di Santa Croce

Calle del Squero

4

A · **B** · **C**

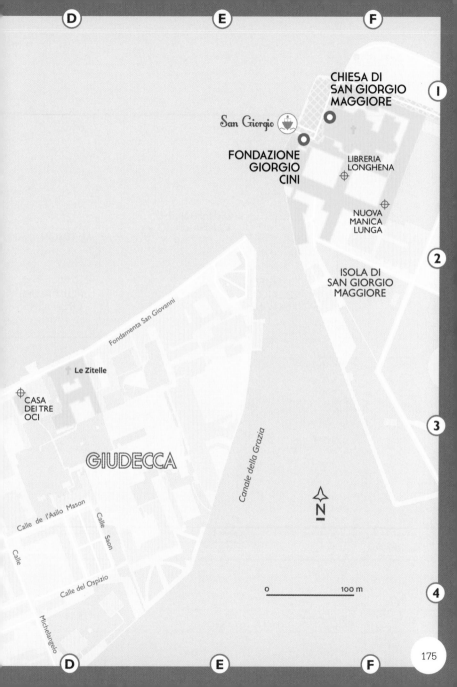

CHIESA DI
SAN GIORGIO
MAGGIORE

San Giorgio

FONDAZIONE
GIORGIO
CINI

LIBRERIA
LONGHENA

NUOVA
MANICA
LUNGA

ISOLA DI
SAN GIORGIO
MAGGIORE

Fondamenta San Giovanni

Le Zitelle

CASA
DEI TRE
OCI

GIUDECCA

Calle de l'Asilo Mason

Calle Saon

Calle

Calle del Ospizio

Michelangelo

Canale della Grazia

N

0   100 m

D   E   F

I

2

3

4

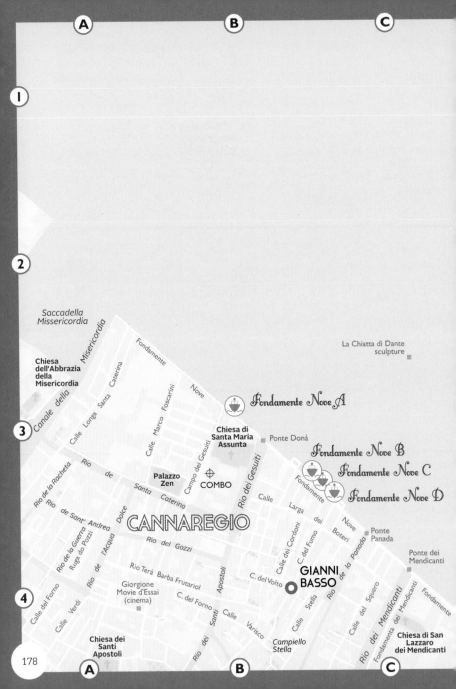

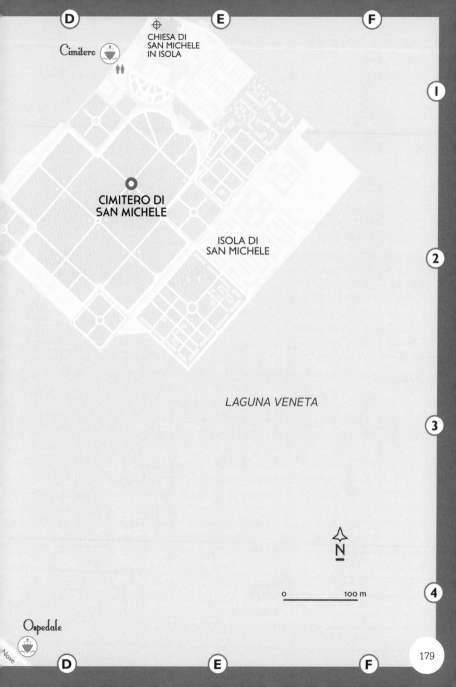

A · B · C

1

Campo
San Bernardo

Calle del Cristo

Canale

Venier

Canale degli Angeli

Fondamenta Venier

Serenella

Calle Alvise Vivarini

Calle Quirizio da Murano

Ramo da Mula

Da Mula

Calle dal Mio

Palazzo
da Mula

Ponte Longo

2

MURANO

TRATTORIA
BUSA ALLA
TORRE

Chiesa di
San Pietro
Martire

Campo Santo
Stefano

Ponte
San Pietro
Martire

Vetrai

Manin

Corte
Alessandro
Turella

Calle A. Zecchin detto Procondio

3

Campiello
Italo
Svevo

Cipriano

Ramo

San

Calle

Bertolini

Calle Bertolini

Campiello de
la Pescheria

ELLEELLE

Fondamenta

Fondamenta

Corte
Bigaglia

Bressagio

Bertolini

Calle

Fondamenta del

Rio

Vetrai

Manin

Calle

Miotti

Calle de l'Ogio

4

Calle

CESARE
TOFFOLO

Fondamenta

Ponte
Santa
Chiara

A · B · C

BASILICA DEI
SS MARIA E
DONATO

OSTERIA AL
DUOMO

MUSEO DEL VETRO
(MUSEUM OF GLASS)

SOTTOVENTO

Campo
San
Donato

Ponte
San
Donato

Fondamenta Lorenzo Radi

Fondamenta Antonio Colleoni

Riva   Longa

Museo

Navagero

Faro di Murano
(lighthouse)

Murano
Faro

Calle de le Conterie

Calle

Fondamenta Marco

Giustinian

Canale di

Fondamenta

San   Antonio

Donato

Macchio

Calle San Giacomo

Grande

di

Murano

Batutti

dei

Giovanni

Fondamenta

Fondamenta Andrea Navagero

Calle Briati

Fondamenta
Francesco M.Piave

Canale

Canale dei Marani

Ondello

Canale

0   100 m

N

181

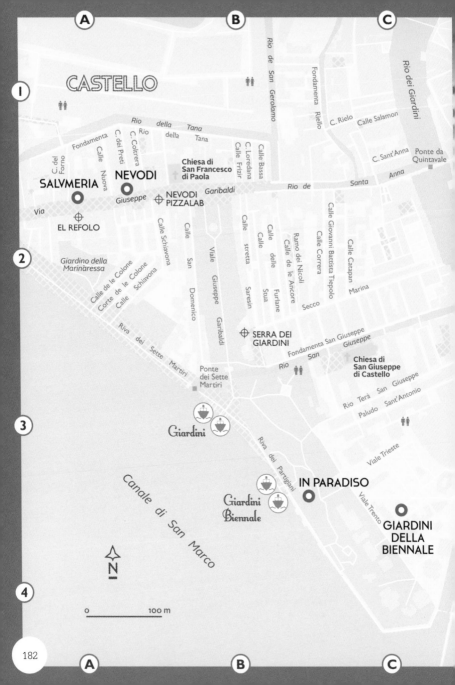

TORCELLO

MUSEO
PROVINCIALE

Canale di Torcello

CHIESA DI
SANTA
FOSCA

BASILICA
DI SANTA
MARIA
ASSUNTA

TAVERNA
TIPICA
VENEZIANA

Maggiore

Canale

Torcello

Canale S. Piereto

Canale Sant'Antonio

ISOLA DEI
LAGHI

Borgononi

N

0   200 m

ISOLA
MAZZORBETTO

Canale di Mazzorbo

Canale

Mazzorbo

VENISSA
RISTORANTE
& OSTERIA

Burano

Burano

MAZZORBO

PANIFICIO
PASTICCERIA
CARMELINA
PALMISANO

BURANO

DALLA
LIDIA

EMILIA
BURANO

MUSEO DEL MERLETTO

ALESSANDRO
TAGLIAPIETRA

ALESSANDRO
TAGLIAPIETRA

CHIESA DI
SAN MARTINO

OSTERIA
AL MUSEO

A   B   C

INDEX

ABOUT THE AUTHOR

Following on from his book *Rome Precincts* published by Hardie Grant Travel, travel writer Cristian Bonetto turns the spotlight on Venice: a city trodden by millions but well known by few. That Venice keeps its cards close to its chest is what Cristian loves most about the place. Every sojourn uncovers new layers and secret locations, far removed from the overpriced, overcrowded Venice deluding the masses. Given that Cristian's father was born and raised in the Veneto region, it's only natural that Venice feels like home for the Australian-born travel writer. Everything from the dialect to the cooking reminds him of his childhood, one coloured with Venetian anecdotes, flavours and pride.

Cristian began his writing life as a playwright running a small theatre company and producing a handful of comedies. In 2003, his play *Il Cortile* (The Courtyard) was awarded an Australia Council grant, leading to its performance in various Italian cities. After a short stint writing scripts for Australian soaps *Home and Away* and *Neighbours*, Cristian turned his hand to travel writing. Since 2006, he has written close to 50 guides for Lonely Planet for destinations as varied as Italy, Scandinavia, the USA, Singapore and his beloved hometown Melbourne. He is also a contributor to UK newspaper, *The Telegraph*.

ACKNOWLEDGEMENTS

A big Venetian *grassie* (thank you) to series creator and publisher Melissa Kayser for entrusting me with the first edition of *Venice Pocket Precincts*. Many thanks also to project editor Megan Cuthbert for her ongoing support, and to meticulous editor Alice Barker for giving my words a thorough workout.

In Italy, much gratitude to the friends, relatives and strangers who shared their passion for Venice and the Veneto region with me. A special shout out to Stefano Baldan, Gian Luca Tumino, Marisa Convento, Audrey Di Fruscia, Alberto Perini, Eky Elisabetta Chiappino, Sabrina Crawford, Max De Martino, Carmelo Grasso, Silvia Vendramin and Marco Guerra, Giovanna Vendramin, Laura Durante, Francesca Sartor and family, as well as Alessandro Merlin.

Back home, thanks to my family and friends for their support, especially to my mother Antonietta for her assistance. Finally, thank *you* for trusting me as your guide through La Serenissima.

Published in 2021 by Hardie Grant Travel,
a division of Hardie Grant Publishing

Hardie Grant Travel (Melbourne)
Wurundjeri Country
Building 1, 658 Church Street
Richmond, Victoria 3121

Hardie Grant Travel (Sydney)
Gadigal Country
Level 7, 45 Jones Street
Ultimo, NSW 2007

www.hardiegrant.com/au/travel

The maps in this publication incorporate
data from:
© OpenStreetMap contributors
OpenStreetMap is made available under the
Open Data Commons Open Database License
(ODbL) by the OpenStreetMap Foundation
(OSMF):
http://opendatacommons.org/licenses/odbl/1.0/.
Any rights in individual contents of the database
are licensed under the Database Contents
License: http://opendatacommons.org/licenses/
dbcl/1.0/
Data extracts via Geofabrik GmbH
https://www.geofabrik.de
© Comune di Venezia – data made available
under the Italian Open Data Licence IODL 2.0

A catalogue record for this book is available from the National Library of Australia

Hardie Grant acknowledges the Traditional
Owners of the Country on which we work,
the Wurundjeri people of the Kulin Nation
and the Gadigal people of the Eora Nation, and
recognises their continuing connection to the
land, waters and culture. We pay our respects
to their Elders past, present and emerging.

Venice Pocket Precincts
ISBN 9781741176513

10 9 8 7 6 5 4 3 2 1

Publisher
Melissa Kayser

Cartographer
Emily Maffei

Project editor
Megan Cuthbert

Design
Michelle Mackintosh

Editor
Alice Barker

Typesetting
Megan Ellis

Proofreader
Judith Bamber

Index
Max McMaster

Colour reproduction by Megan Ellis and
Splitting Image Colour Studio

Printed in Singapore by 1010 Printing
International Limited

Disclaimer: While every care is taken to
ensure the accuracy of the data within this
product, the owners of the data do not make
any representations or warranties about its
accuracy, reliability, completeness or suitability
for any particular purpose and, to the extent
permitted by law, the owners of the data
disclaim all responsibility and all liability
(including without limitation, liability in
negligence) for all expenses, losses, damages
(including indirect or consequential damages)
and costs which might be incurred as a result
of the data being inaccurate or incomplete in
any way and for any reason.

Publisher's Disclaimers: The publisher
cannot accept responsibility for any errors or
omissions. The representation on the maps of
any road or track is not necessarily evidence
of public right of way. The publisher cannot be
held responsible for any injury, loss or damage
incurred during travel. It is vital to research any
proposed trip thoroughly and seek the advice
of relevant state and travel organisations before
you leave.

Publisher's Note: Every effort has been
made to ensure that the information in this
book is accurate at the time of going to press.
The publisher welcomes information and
suggestions for correction or improvement.

POCKET PRECINCTS SERIES

COLLECT THE SET!

Curated guidebooks offering the best cultural, eating and drinking spots to experience the city as the locals do. Each guidebook includes detailed maps at the back and a field trip section encouraging you to venture further afield.

These compact guides are perfect for slipping into your back pocket before you head out on your next adventure.

ADELAIDE · HANOI · HONG KONG · KYOTO · LOS ANGELES · MELBOURNE · MONTRÉAL & QUÉBEC CITY

LONDON · PARIS · SINGAPORE · SAN FRANCISCO · STOCKHOLM · TOKYO · HAVANA

LISBON · OSAKA · VENICE

COMING SOON

KYOTO · NEW YORK & WASHINGTON D.C. · PRAGUE · REYKJAVIK · TEL AVIV · AMSTERDAM · BERLIN

EDINBURGH · BUENOS AIRES · BALI